THE WAY WE UNBOX TALENT

A Corporate Cheerleader's Guide to Talent Review and Succession Planning

---

Sara Bovey Covey

Published by The Corporate Cheerleader

For permissions and inquiries, visit www.thecorporatecheerleader.com

First edition, 2026

Contents

READER'S NOTE

A note for you—before we begin.

Before we begin, I want to let you know I'm here for you—the person who chose to open this book whether out of curiosity, responsibility, excitement, or a little bit of "Oh no... Talent Review season is coming!" Wherever you're starting from, I'm genuinely glad you're here.

I know Talent Review often feels intimidating or maybe even frustrating. For some, just thinking about it drudges up memories of rushed conversations and unclear expectations or maybe feeling the need to squeeze your people into boxes not reflecting who they really are. Others simply always believe there's a better, more human way to do it, one honoring both the business and the people behind the work.

Maybe you're new to this entirely, still working out what Talent Review is supposed to accomplish and whether you're doing it anywhere close to right. If that's you, this book was written with you specifically in mind.

Wherever you're starting from, this book is designed to meet you there—and move toward something better, not heavier.

Remember: Talent Review isn't about mastering a matrix or checking a box but instead leading with clarity, equity, courage, and care. It's about truly seeing people as you learn the skills and mindsets that'll help you evaluate your team more accurately—supporting development in a responsible way—and building a practice that helps your employees grow rather than leave them guessing.

I wrote this book because I believe in leaders who want to do right by their people. Leaders who…

- Believe potential exists beyond what's immediately visible
- Want to challenge bias, build equity, and develop talent with intention
- Crave more confidence walking into these conversations (and more clarity walking out)

As you read, I'd ask one thing: resist the urge to skip to the parts that feel most urgent and treat the rest as optional. The leaders who get the most from this work are the ones who let the full picture form before deciding what to change. You don't need to know everything before you begin. You just need to be willing to look more carefully than you have before.

You will find guidance, tools, structure, and language here. You will also find something less common in books about process: a genuine belief that Talent Review, done well, is an act of care—not just a leadership responsibility.

Thank you for being here, choosing to learn, and showing up for your people in a way not every leader will. Not just reading a book, you're reshaping how you lead—which matters way more than you know.

With cheer (and pom-poms),
Sara Bovey Covey
Your Corporate Cheerleader

PREFACE

My relationship with Talent Review did not begin in a textbook.

I have sat at five different sides of the Talent Review table across four organizations ranging from one hundred to ten thousand employees. I know this process the way a practitioner knows it—not from research alone, but from being in the room, being discussed in the room, and being responsible for what happens after the room clears.

Specifically, I have been—

- The employee being calibrated, sitting outside a closed door while a room full of leaders decided what I was capable of and where I should go next
- The manager preparing profiles, gathering evidence, and trying to advocate clearly for people whose contributions I understood better than anyone else in that room
- The HR business partner facilitating calibration sessions, redirecting bias, and helping leaders find language precise enough to be useful and fair enough to be trusted
- The process designer building talent frameworks from scratch—deciding which models to use, which definitions to anchor, and which structural safeguards would keep the conversation honest when the room got difficult
- The calibration panel member watching, in real time, how quickly a single room can sharpen or distort what an organization thinks it knows about its own people

That range of perspective is what this book is built on. Not theory, not a single vantage point, not one organization's way of doing things—but the accumulated understanding of what Talent Review actually looks like when it works, when it fails, and when the difference between those two outcomes comes down to a single leader asking a better question or a facilitator holding the room to a higher standard.

The scale has mattered too. A talent conversation in a hundred-person organization is intimate and fast-moving; the same conversation in a ten-thousand-person organization is political, layered, and consequential in ways that ripple across entire divisions. I have designed processes for both and facilitated rooms containing every variation in between. What I found is that the principles that make Talent Review work are consistent across all of them. The complexity changes. The fundamentals do not.

The data confirmed what the rooms had already shown me. When I surveyed 62 HR and leadership professionals at a major talent management conference, only 12 reported running a structured, well-facilitated Talent Review. Fifteen admitted to what they called "pencil whipping"—completing ratings quickly to satisfy the process without doing the actual work. The rest either skipped it entirely or were unclear on what it was supposed to accomplish. In an environment where organizations invest significantly in leadership development, that gap between intention and execution is striking. It is also fixable.

I have taught Talent Review in leadership development programs, designed calibration processes for organizations rebuilding their talent infrastructure, coached HR partners through their first facilitated sessions, and worked with managers who had run the process for years without ever fully understanding what it was for. In every context, the intervention that produced the most meaningful change was the same:

giving people a clear, honest account of how the process actually works and what it genuinely requires of them.

That is what this book is: a clear, honest account—grounded in practice, built from experience, and written for the people who are trying to do this work well and deserve better than a form to fill out.

A note on scope: this book is written for leaders and HR practitioners working within a single organization—most effectively in small to mid-size environments where a leadership team can gather in one room and calibrate together. It does not attempt to cover the full complexity of enterprise-level talent management across thousands of employees, multiple global regions, or deeply matrixed reporting structures. That is a different book, and it deserves its own treatment. What this book offers is the foundation: the principles, practices, and habits that make Talent Review meaningful at any scale—and that any more complex system must be built on top of to work at all.

Welcome home. Welcome to The Way We Unbox Talent.

CHAPTER ONE

Intent

Talent Review needs clarity—which begins with intent.

Talent Review is meant to be a structured and intentional conversation about people: their strengths, aspirations, opportunities, and readiness for whatever the organization needs next. It tasks leaders with stepping out of the day-to-day grind as they look at their teams with clarity, honesty, and responsibility. When done well, it is one of the most powerful practices a leadership team has.

Turns out, Talent Review itself isn't the problem; the problem is too many leaders were never taught how powerful this practice can be when treated with intention and care. Without clarity, it becomes a chore. Without skill, it becomes inconsistent. Without purpose, it becomes less impactful.

Before we go any further, let's get rid of all the noise surrounding Talent Review. Here's what it's not…

- A performance review
- A ranking contest
- A verdict on someone's worth
- A way to sort people into boxes
- A punishment or shortcut to a promotion
- A way to fill out a nine-box

Beyond just a leadership responsibility, it provides the chance to understand your people fully—not partially, hurriedly, or based on instinct alone. In this way, leaders can identify who's thriving, who needs support, where potential is emerging, and where future gaps might hinder the organization if not addressed in the here and now.

All of this reminds me of something that happened years ago and shaped my belief in this work. I was facilitating a Talent Review when a leader described an employee as "not strategic… just not leadership material." The room nodded, ready to move on, but not me. I asked: "What evidence do you have supporting that?" Silence.

After what seemed like hours, another leader spoke up: "I've admittedly only seen her under pressure and notice she gets straight to the point. Maybe we're mistaking urgency for lack of strategy."

When we took a step back and reviewed her work, the truth came out (as it always seems to do): she was an incredibly strategic thinker. Within months, she was leading a major initiative and thriving. Had we not questioned the assumptions in the room, her path might have looked entirely different.

Without intention, people get mislabeled.
Without structure, talent stays hidden.
Without development planning, organizations become reactive.
Without challenging assumptions, bias grows.
Without shared understanding, succession pipelines crumble.

When leaders show up fully, though—prepared, honest, curious, and ready to see their people clearly—the impact is immediate and immense. Not only do they make informed decisions, but employees feel supported, organizations gain clarity regarding strengths, risks, and readiness, succession plans materialize, and culture ultimately shifts because people feel the difference even if they never step foot inside the Talent Review room.

This chapter is called "Intent" because this is precisely what transforms Talent Review from an administrative cycle into a meaningful leadership practice rooted in fairness, accountability, and care. Intention means…

The tools matter.
The process matters.
The structure matters.

To make this process the powerful tool it's meant to be, we need to start here: with a commitment to seeing people clearly, developing them intentionally, and prepping our organizations for what comes next. At the heart of Talent Review, this intention lays the foundation for everything that follows.

Veridian Solutions is a mid-size professional services firm—about four hundred employees across four regional offices. For the better part of a decade, their annual Talent Review had worked roughly the same way: department heads emailed ratings to HR in the weeks before a leadership offsite, the CPO (Chief People Officer) glanced at the results, and succession planning was, in Marcus's own words, "a spreadsheet nobody trusted."

Marcus had built the company's operations function before moving into the CPO role. He was not indifferent to people development—

he cared about his teams and showed it. But he was a man who measured success in concrete outcomes, and Talent Review had never produced one he could point to. People were assessed. Nothing much changed. The spreadsheet got updated. The cycle repeated.

What changed his mind was not a book or a consultant. It was losing two people in the same quarter—both of them flagged as succession risks in that spreadsheet—to competitors who had done a better job of telling them they mattered. Marcus had looked at their departure interviews and found the same phrase in both: "I didn't think anyone here was paying attention."

He called Priya, his HR business partner, the week after the second departure. "I want to do this differently," he said. "Not just a new form. Actually differently. Tell me what that looks like."

That conversation is where this cycle started. Not with a framework or a template, but with a CPO asking an honest question and an HR partner willing to give an honest answer. The answer, as Priya told it, was simple in principle and demanding in practice: Talent Review works when leaders show up with intention—which means clarity about the people they're discussing, honesty about what they see, and a genuine commitment to do something with what they learn.

"That's it?" Marcus said.

"That's most of it," Priya said. "The rest is structure."

CHAPTER TWO

How It Started (and How It Broke)

Talent Review hasn't failed; organizations have lost sight of its purpose.

It didn't start as a complicated process. Long before nine-box grids, calibration sessions, and modern leadership models ever came into the picture, Talent Review existed as something simple: leaders gathering to talk about their people. It was driven by necessity in the early days, with organizations needing to know who was capable of stepping into leadership when the company grew, who could take on more responsibility when given the chance, and who needed support to reach their potential. These conversations were practical, human, and often personal. Not about rating people, they were about preparing them.

As organizations grew, leadership structures expanded, and industries became more complex, the need for a more consistent Talent Review process grew with them. Companies began adopting more formal systems to ensure fairness, predictability, and alignment and also introduced relevant tools—not to replace human judgment but to guide it. Calibration created shared language, succession planning became a strategic necessity, and various instruments (e.g., the nine-box matrix) helped leaders quickly visualize patterns in performance and potential.

Somewhere along the way, though, we lost the very essence of what Talent Review is all about. What had begun as a meaningful practice evolved into a convoluted process that then devolved into an irksome task. Leaders who once gathered to better understand their people began rushing through conversations or skipping them entirely. The new focus? The tool instead of the intent. The same people Talent Review set out to serve—employees with careers, goals, and potential—felt and suffered the corresponding consequences.

Part of the shift here is rooted in organizational change, with many companies becoming more data-driven, metric-heavy, and efficiency-focused over time. Talent Review, in turn, picked up additional layers loaded with tools, templates, ratings, and meetings—but not clarity. While all of these extras created structure, they also created confusion. Leaders learned how to fill out forms but not how to evaluate talent; HR learned how to run meetings but not facilitate honest conversations; busy executive teams learned how to "get through it" but not how to actually use it.

Many leaders disengaged as the process became more complex, with Talent Review transforming into a task simply performed for HR rather than something they did for their teams. This same shift—from ownership to obligation—is where the break really happened, not just operational but also cultural.

Talent Review, for example, became misunderstood over time as leaders began confusing it with performance reviews: assuming it was just another ratings exercise. Employees heard about nine-box placements and feared the labels. Some organizations used it as a way to justify decisions rather than plan development, while others failed to have honest conversations in order to prevent conflict. Bias filled in the gaps, meanwhile, wherever clarity was missing. Now, all of this isn't to say leaders didn't care; Talent Review fizzled because they simply weren't taught how to best use it nor shown the purpose behind it.

All of these patterns have become crystal clear in my conversations with HR folks over the years, including the dozens I interviewed at the aforementioned conference. When Talent Review is absent, it's not because it lacks value but because it lacks consistency, clarity, accountability, and confidence. Leaders don't shun it because they don't care about developing people; they simply doubt their ability to evaluate potential, fear getting it wrong, and/or feel overwhelmed by the process.

Another component responsible for breaking Talent Review is organizations that treat tools as the process itself rather than supplementary materials—the nine-box as the conversation rather than one pixel in a much larger picture, and succession planning as a document rather than a promise. When tools are used this way—without intention—they stop being useful.

The general world of work was also changing rapidly, especially across the 2010s and accelerating after 2020 as organizations absorbed faster career movement, distributed teams, shifting skill needs, and a much louder demand for fairness in people decisions. This included…

- People moving between roles and companies more quickly

- Leadership paths becoming less linear
- Skill demands shifting at unprecedented rates
- Remote and hybrid work blurring visibility
- Managers inheriting teams they barely knew
- Underrepresented talent staying underrecognized
- Leaders needing more support than ever to assess talent fairly

The Talent Review cracks widened amidst all of this, leaders relying more heavily on instinct, proximity, and personal comfort—all places where bias tends to thrive—in the absence of a clear framework. Employees, meanwhile, felt this gap.

While the powers that be originally created Talent Review to strengthen organizations and support people, the opposite happens when it's done poorly or not at all: breeding uncertainty, inequity, frustration, and disengagement.

The process is worth rebuilding. Its heart has always been good, its purpose necessary, and its impact transformational—and reclaiming it means reconnecting with the purpose behind the tools, not discarding them.

What Rebuilding Requires

Reclaiming Talent Review does not mean returning to a simpler era or pretending the modern workplace has not changed. It means restoring the original purpose with better tools, clearer standards, and more equitable leadership habits. The work now is to make the conversation structured enough to be fair and human enough to be useful.

A restored Talent Review practice requires leaders to do five things consistently:

1. Separate evidence from instinct.
2. Define performance, potential, and readiness before people are discussed.
3. Examine access, exposure, and sponsorship as part of the conversation.
4. Build development commitments leaders can actually execute.
5. Treat every tool as a prompt for better judgment, not a substitute for it.

That is the throughline of the rest of this book: Talent Review broke when the tool became louder than the purpose. It gets better when leaders put the purpose back in the center.

Before Priya could build something better at Veridian, she needed to understand exactly how the old process had broken—not in theory, but in practice. So she did something most HR partners skip: she went back through five years of talent ratings and cross-referenced them with actual outcomes.

What she found was not malice. It was drift. The ratings had started as genuine assessments and somewhere around year three had become a ritual. Leaders submitted numbers because numbers were requested. The definitions of performance and potential had never been written down, which meant six leaders were using six different mental models. One department head rated almost everyone a four out of five because he didn't believe in giving fives and didn't want to hurt anyone with threes. Another rated half her team as high potential because, as she later admitted to Priya, "I thought that's what you were supposed to do with your best people."

The succession plan had been built on those ratings. Which meant it had been built on noise.

Two of the three people listed as succession-ready for senior roles in the prior year's plan had since left the company. One had been promoted into a role she wasn't ready for and had resigned six months later. A fourth—Darius, a senior project lead in Dominique's department—had been consistently rated high potential for two consecutive cycles and had received exactly zero development actions in that time. He was still there, but Priya had seen the signs. He was looking.

Priya brought this to Marcus not as an indictment but as a diagnosis. "The process didn't fail because people didn't care," she told him. "It failed because the process itself gave them nothing to care about. No shared language. No real accountability. No follow-through built in." Marcus looked at the data for a long moment. "So we rebuild it," he said. "Where do we start?"

CHAPTER THREE

Talent Review Nuts & Bolts

Tools don't make it work—leaders do. But leaders still need to choose the right tool.

The best Talent Review process on the planet doesn't start with forms, templates, or grids. It starts with clarity about the people you're discussing and the purpose behind the conversation. Tools exist to support that clarity—not to replace judgment, assign labels, or make the process feel like a compliance ritual.

This chapter covers the core elements of a meaningful Talent Review: talent profiles, the distinction between performance and potential, talent models, readiness levels, and succession planning. All of them are lenses—ways of seeing your people more clearly.

One of those lenses—the talent model—is where most organizations get stuck. Not because the models are hard to understand, but because there are too many of them and no one wants to commit. This chapter commits.

Talent Profiles: A Strong Talent Review Prerequisite

A talent profile essentially says: "Here's what we know and what we're observing." Not a résumé, performance review, or list of tasks, it gives the room enough context to evaluate someone fairly without overwhelming leaders with noise, answering these questions:

- What does this person consistently do well?

- How do they show up?
- Where is growth happening?
- What do they want next?
- What experiences have shaped them?
- What risks or gaps need attention?

The talent profile is ultimately a leveling mechanism. When it's filled out thoughtfully, it reduces bias, surfaces strengths that might otherwise go unnoticed, and grounds the conversation in evidence rather than impressions. It works best when it's short, current, contains specific examples, includes input from the employee, and reflects both performance and potential—not just history.

A strong profile frees everything else up. A weak one—vague, outdated, or leader-only—poisons the conversation before it starts.

Performance and Potential: The Two Lenses Leaders Most Often Confuse

If talent profiles lay the groundwork, "performance" and "potential" are the first two lenses leaders need to apply—and the two they most consistently conflate. The confusion is understandable. Both matter. But they are not the same thing, and treating them as interchangeable is one of the most reliable ways to misplace talented people.

Performance

Performance answers one question: "What has this person delivered, and how consistently?" It reflects impact, behavior, reliability, and the ability to meet or exceed expectations. It is evidence of contribution over time—not volume of work, not likability, not proximity to the leader, and not simply being the person the leader trusts most.

Potential

Potential answers a different question: "What is the likelihood this person will grow—and to what capacity—with the right support, experiences, and time?" It is about learning agility, adaptability, curiosity, and the ability to influence beyond the current role. It is a bet on trajectory.

Potential is not charisma. It is not confidence. It is not extroversion, convenience, or similarity to the leader. It is not immediate promotability. Leaders who mistake any of those things for potential will systematically over-invest in people who look the part and under-invest in people who are actually on a stronger trajectory.

Getting these two lenses right before picking a talent model matters enormously—because every model on the market is built on some version of these two variables. If the room doesn't share a definition of performance and potential before the conversation starts, the model is just a grid with different people's hunches plotted on it.

The Model Question: Stop Choosing and Start Deciding

Most books on talent management present a buffet of models and tell you to choose what fits your culture. That is not a recommendation; it is an abdication. It puts the hardest decision back in the hands of the reader and calls it empowerment.

So here is an actual recommendation: for most organizations, most of the time, start with the Now/Next model. Not because it is the most sophisticated tool available—it isn't—but because it is the one most likely to produce honest conversations, equitable evaluations, and development plans people actually follow through on. It is also the one least likely to collapse into a ranking exercise when facilitation is imperfect.

There are two other models every organization should understand regardless of which one they use. The Nine-Box because it is unavoidable—it exists in your organization already, or it will—and understanding its failure modes is as important as understanding its mechanics. And the Flight Risk/Critical Value matrix because it is the one model that speaks directly to the question executives care about most: what happens to the business if this person leaves?

Five other models exist and have real value in specific contexts. They are covered in the reference table at the end of this section. But the three below are the ones worth understanding deeply—before you pick up a grid, before you open a meeting, before you put a single name on a whiteboard.

Model One: The Nine-Box Grid—Know It Before You Inherit It

The Nine-Box plots performance on one axis and potential on the other, producing nine categories that range from "low performance, low potential" to "high performance, high potential." It is the most widely used talent model in corporate America. It is also, in the hands of an underprepared leadership team, one of the most reliably damaging ones.

The model is not broken. The way it is typically used is. Three failure patterns repeat so consistently across organizations that they deserve naming before any leader picks up this tool.

The placement becomes the conversation. Leaders spend the meeting deciding which box someone belongs in rather than discussing the evidence, the development need, or the action. The box replaces the point.

"Potential" never gets defined. Without a shared definition, the potential axis becomes a proxy for whoever the leader likes, trusts, or sees most often. The model then measures familiarity, not trajectory.

The box becomes permanent. Employees placed in lower boxes in one cycle rarely get reconsidered in the next, regardless of what has changed. What was meant to be a moment-in-time assessment calcifies into a career ceiling.

The Nine-Box is worth understanding because you will encounter it. Use it only if your team has aligned definitions of both axes before anyone's name is discussed, has a strong enough facilitator to keep placement from becoming the endpoint, and commits to treating placements as revisable—not permanent. If any of those three conditions are missing, the Now/Next model will serve you better.

Model Two: The Now/Next Model—The Recommended Starting Point

The Now/Next model asks two questions: Where is this person now? And where might they go next? The "now" categories are:

Thriving in Role, Needs Targeted Development, and Re-Skill or Reposition. The "next" categories are: Ready for Bigger Scope and Building for Next.

What makes this model the recommended starting point for most organizations is not simplicity alone—though it is simple. It is the structural logic embedded in the two questions. "Where are they now?" requires evidence of current contribution. "Where might they go next?" requires a conversation about development, aspiration, and organizational opportunity. Together they force the room to do exactly what Talent Review is supposed to do: connect a realistic assessment of the present to an intentional plan for the future.

It also has a meaningful equity advantage. Because it is built around conversation rather than coordinates on a grid, it is harder to treat as a ranking exercise. There is no "top box" to compete for. There is only a discussion about where someone is and what would help them grow—which is, at its core, what every employee deserves from this process.

The model has real limitations. It can feel vague if leaders arrive without specific examples. The "next" categories require organizational clarity about what bigger scope actually looks like in your context—and that clarity doesn't always exist. And it is less useful in large, complex organizations where finer differentiation is genuinely needed to drive compensation, succession, and development investment decisions.

But for an organization new to structured Talent Review, or one whose previous process devolved into box-filling and label-assigning, Now/Next is the reset the room needs. It returns the conversation to the people—which is where it was always supposed to be.

Model Three: Flight Risk/Critical Value—The Business Case in a Grid

This model asks two questions that have nothing to do with development and everything to do with organizational risk: How likely is this person to leave? And how painful would it be if they did?

Plotting those two variables produces four quadrants: low flight risk and high critical value (protect and develop), high flight risk and high critical value (intervene now), low flight risk and low critical value (maintain), and high flight risk and low critical value (assess and decide). The action in each quadrant is different, but the discipline is the same: the organization stops reacting to departures and starts anticipating them.

This model matters for a reason the others don't address directly: it speaks the language of business continuity. When a CFO, a board member, or a risk-focused CEO asks why Talent Review deserves organizational investment, the answer isn't "because it's the right thing to do for people." The answer is: the average cost of an unplanned leadership vacancy runs between 50 and 200 percent of the departing leader's annual salary once recruiting, lost productivity, team disruption, and institutional knowledge loss are accounted for. The Flight Risk/Critical Value matrix is the tool that translates that risk into a list of names and a set of actions—which is exactly what a board-level conversation about talent requires.

It has weaknesses. Without psychological safety in the room, flight risk assessments become guesswork or wishful thinking. Leaders may understate risk for employees they don't want to lose and overstate it for employees they would be relieved to see go. And the model can tip into fear-driven retention decisions that preserve headcount without actually investing in people.

Used well—honestly, with current data, in a room with enough trust to name real concerns—it is one of the most valuable tools a leadership team has. Used poorly, it becomes an anxiety exercise. The difference, as with every model in this chapter, is the quality of the conversation the tool produces.

The Other Five: A Reference Guide

Five additional models have genuine value in the right context. None of them are the right starting point for most organizations, but each addresses something the three models above do not. The table below summarizes when each earns its place.

16-Box Model (Expanded Performance + Potential). Use when your Nine-Box culture has matured and leaders need finer differentiation to drive compensation and succession decisions in large, complex organizations. Requires strong facilitation and experienced leadership teams. Prone to the same failure modes as the Nine-Box, amplified.

Impact/Potential Matrix. Use when output metrics don't capture real contribution—in service, innovation, or collaborative roles where influence matters as much as deliverables. Replaces "performance" with "impact," which is more meaningful but harder to measure objectively. Equity depends on strong, specific examples.

Growth Trajectory Model. Use in fast-moving environments where momentum matters more than current standing. Categories (Accelerating, Steady, Stalled, Rebounding, At Risk) capture direction of travel rather than a static snapshot. Particularly useful for surfacing burnout risk early. Requires ongoing observation—not just annual reviews.

Narrative-Based Assessment. Use in small, relational organizations where nuance matters more than calibration at scale. No grid, no placement—just a structured written summary across six dimensions. Human and richly detailed, but time-consuming and difficult to calibrate across teams. Works best when a skilled facilitator can hold the conversation accountable to evidence.

Capability-Future Potential Matrix. Use when you have a functioning competency model that leaders actually reference—not one that lives in a handbook nobody reads. Evaluates current leadership behaviors against future potential, making assessments clearer and more objective. Collapses entirely if the competency model is undefined or ignored.

Readiness Levels: Bringing Time Into the Mix

Whichever model you use, readiness is the variable that brings time into the equation. Readiness is not a measure of worth—it is a measure of timing. An employee who is not ready for expanded scope today may be the strongest succession candidate in two years. Treating "not ready" as "not capable" is one of the most common and most costly misreadings a leadership team can make.

Common readiness levels: Ready Now, Ready Soon (12–24 months), Ready Later (2–5 years), Developing (foundational growth needed), and Thriving in Role (no movement desired or warranted). A healthy process treats all five as legitimate and useful—not as a hierarchy where only Ready Now counts.

Readiness is only useful when it is paired with a development commitment. A readiness assessment without a corresponding action plan is just a label with a timeline attached.

Succession Planning: The Strategy Steering the Ship

If Talent Review is the engine, succession planning is the navigation system. It answers a question organizations ask too rarely and too late: "If this role becomes open tomorrow, who is truly ready to step in—and what would they need to succeed?"

A succession plan is not an org chart with penciled-in names. It is a living risk-mitigation strategy that reflects which roles are critical, who could step in, what evidence supports their readiness, what experiences they still need, where single points of failure exist, whether the pipeline reflects equity and future skill needs, and which development must happen before the next opportunity arrives.

Organizations with weak succession pipelines are slower to respond to market shifts, more vulnerable to key-person risk, and more likely to promote reactively—placing the person who happened to be available rather than the person who was prepared. That is not a talent problem. It is a business problem with a talent solution.

Great succession planning doesn't require certainty about who will leave or when. It requires honesty about who is developing, evidence about their readiness, and courage to have the conversations that keep the plan current. The leaders who avoid it because it feels presumptuous or premature are the ones who find themselves making the most consequential organizational decisions under the most pressure, with the least preparation.

Tying It All Together

A complete Talent Review pulls together five things: a talent profile (the person), performance and potential (the lenses), a talent model (the structure), readiness levels (the timing), and succession planning (the strategy). Every element depends on the others. A talent profile without a model is rich but inconsistent. A model without a profile is structured but blind. Readiness without succession is a data point with nowhere to go.

The recommendation stands: start with Now/Next, layer in Flight Risk/Critical Value when the business case needs to be made or retention is a live concern, and understand the Nine-Box well enough to recognize when it is working and when it is quietly producing the same ranking exercise it was designed to prevent.

And remember what the tools are for. Not to classify people. Not to build a permanent record of who was impressive in a single conversation. To make it easier for leaders to see clearly, talk honestly, and do something useful with what they learn. The model is never the point. The people are.

When Priya sat down with Marcus to choose a model for Veridian's rebuilt process, she put three options in front of him. The Nine-Box, which he already knew. A more complex matrix she thought would eventually suit Veridian but not yet. And the Now/Next model, which she recommended for where they were starting from.

"The Nine-Box is the one everyone knows," she told him, "which is also its biggest problem. People think they understand it before anyone defines the axes, and then you get six leaders in a room with six different ideas of what 'high potential' means. You've seen what that produces—it's in the data I showed you."

"Now/Next is simpler," she continued. "Two questions: where is this person now, and where might they go next? The model forces the conversation toward development rather than placement. It's harder to turn into a ranking exercise. And for a team that's never had a structured calibration conversation before, it gives them something concrete to react to without overwhelming them."

Marcus asked the question Priya had expected: "Does simpler mean less rigorous?"

"It means the rigor comes from the conversation rather than the grid," she said. "Which is exactly where it should come from."

They agreed on Now/Next. Marcus drafted the one-page guide that would go to all six department heads six weeks before the meeting—not a process manual, but a clear statement of what Talent Review was for, what model they'd be using, and what definition of potential the team had agreed on: learning agility, adaptability, and the ability to influence beyond one's immediate role.

That definition would prove to be one of the most important decisions they made. Not because it was perfect, but because it was shared.

CHAPTER FOUR

Dealing with Bias

When partiality goes unchallenged, potential goes unseen.

Bias is one of the most uncomfortable Talent Review topics, not because people don't care about it but because most of us were never taught how to recognize it in real time—let alone interrupt it with confidence and grace. Not a flaw in character, it's a feature of the human brain. We're wired to take mental shortcuts, rely on familiarity, and fill in gaps with what feels authentic rather than what's proven. It's normal, human, and exactly why intention and structure are Talent Review need-to-haves.

Wanting fairness and producing fairness are two different things. Good intentions don't automatically protect people from bias—clear processes, shared language, and practiced awareness do.

When bias shows up, it doesn't do so in a dramatic or obvious way and is typically wrapped in language that sounds pretty reasonable. It happens when…

- Someone says "She's just not leadership material" without mentioning any specifics
- A leader praises someone who reminds them of themselves
- Confidence is mistaken for competence, quiet is mistaken for lack of ambition, and comfort is mistaken for potential
- Employee growth is ignored due to a misstep a year earlier, or overestimated due to a strong first impression

Bias isn't always about identity. Sometimes it's about style, tenure, and proximity: who's seen most often, speaks the loudest, presents well in meetings, or is easiest to reach. Talent Review brings these patterns to the surface, not to judge leaders but to help them grow.

Dealing with bias effectively means first acknowledging a cold hard fact: everyone has bias. The difference? Whether or not we let our own biases drive our decisions. Recognizing bias isn't about blame; it's about accountability and leaders owning the responsibility they carry while evaluating someone's future.

The most common types of Talent Review biases are also the most predictable:

- "Like-me bias," which shows up when leaders favor those sharing their personality, background, work style, or communication preferences
- "Proximity bias," which surfaces in hybrid and remote settings whereby the people leaders see most often are the ones they believe they know best
- "Recency bias," which causes leaders to overemphasize their most recent interactions or challenges
- "Confidence bias," which sees leaders rewarding polished communication over actual capability
- "Halo" or "horn" bias, which results in allowing one strong or weak trait to color the entire assessment

These patterns have been documented in organizational research for decades. In a foundational study, Pulakos and Wexley (1983) found that perceptual similarity between managers and subordinates accounted for a statistically significant portion of performance rating variance—employees who were seen as similar to their managers received meaningfully higher appraisals than those who were not. [1] The halo effect—the tendency to let one strong or weak trait color an entire assessment—was first documented by Thorndike as early as 1920, who found that raters were systematically unable to evaluate traits independently of their overall impression of a person.[2] Both effects are not signs of careless leadership. They are features of how human judgment operates under conditions of incomplete information and social proximity.

These patterns don't mean leaders are careless; they're just human. Talent Review doesn't serve to eliminate bias entirely—that's impossible—but to interrupt it, reduce its impact, and swap assumptions for evidence.

Interrupting bias need not be confrontational; it can be gentle, curious, and grounded in the intention of the room thanks to phrases like…

- "What evidence supports that?"
- "Can you please share a recent example?"
- "Is what you said based on style or performance?"
- "Has this employee had the same opportunities as others?"
- "How much of this is visibility versus contribution?"
- "What strengths are we missing by focusing only on that one thing?"

These questions don't accuse but illuminate, moving the conversation from assumption to understanding.

[1] Wexley, K. N., & Pulakos, E. D. (1983). The Effects of Perceptual Congruence and Sex on Subordinates' Performance Appraisals of Their Managers. *Academy of Management Journal, 26*(4), 666–676. https://doi.org/10.5465/255914

[2] Thorndike, E. L. (1920). A constant error in psychological ratings. *Journal of Applied Psychology, 4*(1), 25-29. https://doi.org/10.1037/h0071663

One of the most powerful ways to reduce bias is to ensure the conversation is rooted in evidence. Clear and thoughtfully prepared talent profiles help here, grounding the room, with leaders prepared with real examples to shift discussions away from personal impressions and toward observable behavior. Calibration (discussed in detail in the next chapter) is another bias-reduction tool, giving leaders different perspectives and inviting colleagues to challenge each other—not out of criticism but out of a commitment to fairness.

Perhaps the most important way to reduce bias is to create a culture where leaders feel comfortable changing their minds and can say "Ya know what? I hadn't considered that" without losing credibility. If we want leaders to evaluate talent fairly, we need to encourage them to practice humility—and reward the same.

Silence, avoidance, rushing, and certainty are what break it. The goal isn't to catch leaders doing something wrong but to help them do something right—evaluate people with clarity, consistency, and compassion.

> *Clarity helps everyone: employees feel more supported, leaders feel more confident, organizations make better decisions, and culture strengthens because fairness is no longer accidental but very much intentional.*

Priya scheduled thirty-minute prep calls with each of the six department heads in the two weeks before the meeting. These calls were not administrative. They were intelligence-gathering—and they were where bias showed up first, before a single name had been discussed in the calibration room.

She asked each leader three questions: Who on your team do you feel most confident evaluating, and why? Who do you feel least confident about, and why? And where do you think your own blind spots might be in this process?

The third question was the one that mattered most. Most leaders deflected it initially—"I try to be fair," or "I think I know my team pretty well." But a few paused and said something honest. One admitted she tended to rate people more generously after a strong quarter regardless of the longer pattern. Another said he realized he had far more evidence for his in-office team members than for the two people who worked remotely. He hadn't thought about what that meant until Priya asked.

Two leaders—Dominique and Rafael—gave nearly identical responses. Both expressed confidence about their teams. Both, when Priya reviewed their completed talent profiles, had clustered almost everyone in the middle categories. Neither had named a single person as Ready for Bigger Scope. Neither had flagged a single person as needing targeted development. Priya noted this carefully. Clustering in the middle is rarely an accurate picture of a team. It is usually a picture of a leader who hasn't thought hard enough—or who is conflict-averse enough to avoid either strong endorsement or difficult conversations.

She didn't call this out on the prep calls. She noted it and brought it into the room. The most powerful place to interrupt a pattern is not the phone call before the meeting. It is the moment in the calibration room when another leader offers a different view and the first leader has to decide whether to hold their position or look more closely. That moment was coming. Priya was going to make sure it happened.

CHAPTER FIVE

Calibration

Fairness isn't automatic—it's calibrated.

When Talent Review becomes more than a collection of individual opinions, that's calibration: where leaders come together, compare perspectives, challenge assumptions, and leave the room aligned on what talent looks like in their organization. The process becomes subjective in its absence. In its presence? It becomes fair, placing it at the very heart of what Talent Review is all about.

Every leader naturally evaluates talent through their own lens, shaped by experiences, expectations, communication style, and comfort levels. Even leaders with the very best intentions can have wildly different standards. Where one leader sees "high potential," another may see "solid but steady." These differences aren't wrong; they're human. Yet they can become a problem when organizations allow individual standards to guide decisions driving people's futures.

Calibration is the elixir here.

The power of calibration ultimately lies in its ability to equalize the playing field, preventing one leader's comfort or confidence in an employee from defining that employee's trajectory. It helps uncover hidden talent—people doing exceptional work behind the scenes or in less-visible areas—and surfaces development needs one particular leader may have overlooked. It also reins in bias as other leaders have the chance to offer evidence, context, or counterpoints. Finally, calibration helps ensure employees are evaluated based on their performance, behaviors, and potential rather than a leader's personal style preference.

I've personally facilitated hundreds of calibration conversations. Leaders typically kick off the meeting confident in their assessments. As the conversation unfolds, however, something shifts. Upon hearing perspectives they hadn't considered, leaders learn about contributions happening outside their line of sight and question assumptions they've long clung to. The room begins to settle into something more honest, balanced, and aligned.

One specific example stands out. During a Talent Review for a large operations team, a leader insisted an employee was "not promotable." Another leader raised their hand and said, "I've worked with her on two cross-functional projects. She absolutely has leadership potential but just doesn't get the same visibility in your department." That one assertive comment changed the trajectory of the entire conversation—not in a combative way but as a reminder that no single leader can see the entire picture. Calibration allows all the pieces to come together.

Effective calibration requires structure beginning with common language and shared definitions—what "high performance" means, what "potential" looks like, and what "ready soon" actually indicates. The more leaders tether themselves to shared language, the more confident and equitable subsequent decisions are.

Calibration also calls for sound preparation whereby leaders arrive with examples, not impressions, and reflect on opportunities employees have and haven't had access to. Just as importantly, calibration requires courage—leaders willing to challenge each other respectfully and provide alternative perspectives. Saying things like "I see it differently" or "Can we talk about the evidence behind that?" isn't a form of conflict but leadership.

When calibration is missing, Talent Review becomes fragmented. Employees in one department are labeled "ready now" while those in another with the same strengths "need development." Bias runs rampant and goes unchecked. Succession planning becomes guesswork, development is inconsistent, and trust erodes because employees know the standard isn't the same for everyone.

Calibration turns Talent Review from a meeting into a team effort. When done well, it doesn't just improve the process; it closes the gap between what one leader sees and what the whole room knows — which is exactly what the next chapter is about.

The calibration meeting at Veridian was scheduled for two and a half hours on a Tuesday morning. All six department heads were present, along with Marcus and Priya. Before a single employee was discussed, Priya spent fifteen minutes on something that looked, from the outside, like throat-clearing: aligning on definitions.

She put three questions on the screen. What does "high performance" mean at Veridian—not in general, but specifically, given the work you actually do? What does "potential" mean—and what does it not mean? And what does "Ready for Bigger Scope" look like in this organization—is it readiness for promotion, for expanded responsibility in the current role, or something else?

The third question produced the most useful collision. Marcus said "promotion." Kenji said "expanded responsibility—those are different things." Dominique said she'd assumed it meant promotion. Rafael looked at his completed profile sheets and said, quietly, that he might have rated some people differently if he'd known they were distinct.

This conversation took fifteen minutes. It was not wasted time. It was the most important fifteen minutes of the entire meeting—because it revealed that six leaders had walked in with six different mental models of the central concept they were about to use to evaluate every employee in the organization. Without that alignment, the calibration session would have produced comparisons between incompatible data points. With it, the room had a shared foundation to build on.

The first forty-five minutes of employee discussions moved efficiently. Where profiles were detailed and evidence was clear, the group aligned quickly. Where profiles were thin, Priya asked questions rather than moving on. Two placements were revised upward based on cross-functional evidence other leaders brought.

One was revised downward—gently, with a development action attached—when it became clear the profile reflected tenure rather than recent contribution.

Then they reached Camille.

CHAPTER SIX

Visibility, Exposure, and Experience Equity

The best talent doesn't always rise on its own. It rises when leaders make room for it.

Let's talk about one of the biggest Talent Review misconceptions out there: the belief that "the best talent always rises." While this notion sounds comforting and almost noble, it creates a dangerous blind spot in practice. Talent doesn't always rise on its own but instead when leaders notice it, nurture it, and carve out chances for it to grow. Far too often, the difference between who rises and who stays invisible has nothing to do with ability and everything to do with access, exposure, and visibility.

Here are some truths Talent Review must confront head-on: Visibility is not the same as value. Exposure is not the same as readiness. Lack of access is not the same as lack of potential.

This is precisely why a fair Talent Review process intentionally looks beyond who's most visible and examines who's perhaps overlooked. When leaders only evaluate the people they know well, they unintentionally reinforce inequity. This is especially true for employees who work in a quieter way, avoid self-promotion, operate in roles away from senior leadership, and report to managers who aren't strong advocates.

Exposure also comes into play here. People given the chance to lead cross-functional work, stretch into new spaces, and/or navigate challenges often look more "ready" in a Talent Review conversation. That same perceived readiness, however, sometimes reflects opportunity rather than capability.

Experience equity is key—giving employees fair access to the types of assignments, interactions, and developmental moments that'll help them grow and gain visibility. This doesn't mean everyone has identical experiences; it means leaders make intentional choices to develop people broadly and fairly by asking questions like…

- Who consistently receives high-impact assignments?
- Who hasn't been given a chance to stretch?
- Who's ready for exposure but needs an invitation to show what they've got?
- Who has exceptional strengths but limited visibility?
- Who's delivering results behind the scenes but not being recognized?

Visibility and experience equity also help isolate the people who need advocacy. While some employees navigate their careers with powerful sponsors (leaders who speak their names when they're not present), others depend on work that speaks for itself—admirable but not enough in large, complex organizations.

I personally once facilitated a Talent Review where a leader said, "I'm surprised she's not already on the succession slate. She's phenomenal!" Someone else piped up: "I don't think we've talked about her enough. Her work is definitely solid, but she hasn't been given the opportunity to lead anything substantial." The room got quiet. The leader responsible for her team realized she'd unintentionally kept her off the radar. A shift followed; she was given a stretch project not six months later, and her confidence soared.

Equity in Talent Review isn't about equal outcomes but instead opportunity. It creates a process recognizing hidden potential and asks leaders to look beyond the usual suspects. Visibility, exposure, and experience equity aren't just Talent Review concepts; they're full-fledged leadership practices shaping culture, influencing retention, and telling employees: "You belong here. You're seen. Your growth matters."

Structural Moves That Make Equity Operational

Good intentions are not an equity strategy. Reducing inequity requires structural practices that force the room to see what habit, proximity, and comfort tend to miss.

Start by reviewing opportunity distribution before evaluating readiness. Who received stretch assignments, executive exposure, crisis work, mentorship, sponsorship, training, flexible support, and decision-making authority over the past year? If those opportunities were uneven, the Talent Review conversation should name that imbalance before deciding who is "ready."

Next, require evidence across more than one context. One manager's view matters, but it should not be the entire story. Cross-functional feedback, project outcomes, employee aspirations, customer impact, peer leadership, and examples from different settings help prevent one narrow perspective from becoming the official narrative.

Finally, build a sponsorship correction into the process. When the room identifies someone with strong contribution but limited visibility, the next step should not be "keep watching." The next step should be an intentional exposure plan: who will sponsor them, what opportunity will increase their visibility, and when the team will revisit progress.

> *A fair process asks more than "Who is ready?" It also asks: who has been prepared, who has been sponsored, and who has been overlooked because the system made their work harder to see?*

Remote and Hybrid Talent Review

Remote and hybrid work make this chapter even more important. When leaders do not see people in the same physical space, visibility can become accidental: the person who speaks most often on video, responds fastest in chat, lives closest to the office, or overlaps most with the leader's time zone can look more engaged even when someone else is producing equal or stronger impact.

In distributed environments, leaders should prepare talent profiles with extra discipline. They need examples from written work, asynchronous collaboration, project outcomes, customer or stakeholder feedback, decision quality, learning agility, and team contribution—not just meeting presence. They should also ask whether time zones, caregiving schedules, site assignments, travel expectations, or technology access have affected visibility.

Hybrid calibration also needs better meeting design. Share materials early. Invite written pre-work. Give leaders time to add evidence before the live meeting. Make room for quieter leaders to contribute in writing during or after the session. And when the group discusses someone whose work is primarily remote, pause before using phrases like "not visible enough" or "hard to read." Those may be clues about the leader's access, not the employee's potential.

The goal is not to lower the bar for remote or hybrid employees. The goal is to stop using office presence as a proxy for readiness.

Rafael presented Camille, an operations manager in his regional group, as "solid—Thriving in Role." When Priya asked for a specific example of her impact, Rafael paused.

"She runs her region well. No complaints."

"What does she do well, specifically? What has she produced or led that we could point to?"

Another pause. "Honestly, she's pretty autonomous. I don't have a lot of visibility into her day-to-day."

The room went quiet in the way rooms do when something true and uncomfortable has been said out loud.

Kenji spoke first. "I've worked with Camille on two cross-regional projects in the last year. She was the one who caught the data discrepancy in Q3 that would have cost us the client. And she trained four people from other regions on the new intake process—without being asked. She identified the gap, built the training, ran it. That's not 'no complaints.' That's initiative."

Priya: "So we have strong cross-functional evidence of problem-solving, proactive development work, and client impact. Rafael—does that change your view?"

Rafael nodded slowly. "Yeah. I think I've been underestimating her because I don't see her often enough."

"That's an honest and important thing to name," Priya said. "The question isn't whether Camille has been performing well—it sounds like she has. The question is whether she's been visible enough for that performance to reach the people who make decisions about her future. Right now, the answer is no. Let's change that."

Camille moved to Ready for Bigger Scope. Rafael committed to a monthly one-on-one and to including her in the next regional leadership briefing. But Priya had already made a note in her facilitation guide: how many others like Camille were in this organization? How many employees were sitting in Thriving in Role not because that was the right assessment but because their manager's limited visibility had quietly become the ceiling of their career?

It was not a comfortable question. It was the right one.

CHAPTER SEVEN

Leadership Accountability

Talent Review isn't an HR exercise but a leadership responsibility.

Leadership accountability here boils down to a few key commitments: preparation, honesty, consistency, evidence, development ownership, and follow-through. Let's discuss each.

Preparation

When a leader walks into Talent Review unprepared, it sends a clear message not about the team but about their values. Not just about filling out forms, preparation means understanding your people deeply enough to speak to their contributions, strengths, challenges, and aspirations: reviewing talent profiles, gathering examples, and reflecting on development progress. Leaders who prepare thoughtfully create trust, whereas those who don't find themselves in a room forced to waste time guessing and scrambling with meaningful decisions sacrificed in the process.

Honesty

Talent Review cannot function if leaders shun honesty out of discomfort. Employees deserve clarity about where they're thriving and where they need support. Leaders who sugarcoat the truth, gloss over development needs, or refuse to articulate concerns put people at risk—not due to the harshness of said concerns but because the absence of clarity stifles employee growth. Honesty, delivered delicately, is one of the most supportive actions a leader can offer.

Consistency

All employees deserve an evaluation based on the same standards, expectations, and definitions rather than who they report to. When one leader holds the team to a much higher bar than all others, employees experience inconsistency, frustration, and inequity. Talent Review becomes political instead of purposeful. Leaders must commit to evaluating people through shared lenses grounded in organizational values and clearly defined expectations.

Evidence

Rooting Talent Review conversations in observable behaviors, documented contributions, and real examples—instead of impressions, assumptions, or memory fragments—is what makes Talent Review fair. Leaders prepared with evidence elevate the conversation, whereas those who avoid specifics create confusion and protect employees from misinterpretation.

Owning Development

Leaders can't walk into Talent Review, describe a development need, leave, and assume someone else will take care of it. Development is a leader-employee partnership benefitting from development plans that are real, resourced, and achievable—not vague promises or recycled goals. It means creating opportunities, not waiting for them to appear, and having a presence in the employee's growth journey instead of outsourcing it.

Follow-Through

Should a leader walk out of a Talent Review energized by the conversation but then never follow up on commitments made, all credibility is lost. Employees feel this gap, particularly when words spoken don't translate into real-life actions. Follow-through builds trust; its absence erodes it.

I remember one particular Talent Review when a leader repeatedly described an employee as "not ready" because she lacked experience in two key areas. Asked to name the development opportunities that would help her gain that experience, the leader just shrugged. Another leader spoke up and mentioned two upcoming projects perfect for the task. The other leader's response? "Well, she's never raised it with me." Everyone was stunned—not because anyone was at fault but because the truth became painfully clear. The employee wasn't underprepared; she was under-sponsored.

Leadership accountability also means challenging bias—both your own and others'. This doesn't mean confronting colleagues harshly; it means asking questions that open possibilities: "Let's look at the full picture," "I'm not sure we've seen enough to make that call," or "Has this person had the same opportunities as others?"

Talent Review works when leaders work—not harder, but with more intention. The preparation, the honesty, the evidence, the follow-through: none of it is complicated. All of it is a choice.

The differences in preparation across Veridian's six department heads were visible before the calibration meeting began. Priya could see it in the profiles.

Kenji's were the benchmark. For each of his twelve direct reports, he had written two to four sentences of specific evidence—not impressions, not adjectives, but things that had actually happened. He had noted career aspirations based on conversations he'd had in one-on-ones over the previous year. He had flagged two employees as potential flight risks and explained, concisely, what he was seeing and what he had already tried. His profiles read like someone who had been paying attention all year and was now being asked to summarize what he knew.

Rafael's were the cautionary contrast. Camille's profile had "strong performer" under strengths and nothing else. Two others had single-sentence observations that Priya could not have traced to any specific moment or behavior. Rafael was not a careless leader—he managed a high-performing region and his team respected him. But his preparation for Talent Review reflected a common and costly assumption: that the things he knew intuitively about his team were sufficient. They weren't. Intuition without evidence is invisible in a calibration room.

When the meeting ended, Priya sat with Marcus for a debrief. She told him that the quality of conversation in the room had been directly proportional to the quality of the profiles leaders had brought. "Kenji's employees got a fair hearing," she said. "A few others got the hearing their manager was prepared to give them. Those aren't the same thing."

Marcus was quiet for a moment. "So preparation is an equity issue," he said.

"It always was," Priya said. "We just hadn't named it that way."

CHAPTER EIGHT

A Healthy Talent Review Culture

Culture is baked into the conversations leaders choose to have and refuse to avoid.

It all starts with psychological safety. Amy Edmondson's foundational research defines it as a shared belief among team members that the environment is safe for interpersonal risk-taking—that speaking up, challenging assumptions, and admitting uncertainty will not be punished.[3] In a Talent Review room, this translates directly: without it, leaders say what they think they should say rather than what is true, avoid naming development needs to steer clear of conflict, and minimize concerns with the belief that accuracy is less important than harmony.

A healthy culture also requires curiosity, keeping leaders from making assumptions and encouraging them to wonder: What might I be missing? Or: Has this person had the chance to show what they're capable of? Curiosity invites leaders to see potential not as a fixed trait but as something dynamic. When it's absent, decisions calcify, creativity dries up, and assumptions go unchallenged.

Respectful candor is also a part of this. Respect without candor is politeness. Candor without respect? Harshness. Leaders who blend the

---

[3] Edmondson, A. (1999). Psychological Safety and Learning Behavior in Work Teams. *Administrative Science Quarterly*, *44*(2), 350–383. https://doi.org/10.2307/2666999

two create conditions where honest conversations about performance, readiness, and development can flourish.

A healthy culture also promotes shared ownership of talent where leaders refuse to operate inside their own silos. Shared ownership means leaders see talent as belonging to the organization (beyond their own department), support someone's development even if it means losing that person to another team, and champion developing people as a collective—not competitive—responsibility.

Transparency in expectations doesn't mean sharing everything with employees but simply being clear about what matters. Employees deserve to know what skills, behaviors, and experiences contribute to readiness, just as much as they deserve ongoing development conversations instead of annual surprises.

A healthy culture also values development over judgment. When organizations treat Talent Review like a contest—with winners moving up and losers getting labeled—they destroy trust. A healthy culture considers Talent Review a tool for growth and views development needs as normal rather than shameful.

The clearest sign of a healthy Talent Review culture is how leaders talk about employees when they're not in the room. In strong cultures, the tone is respectful, thoughtful, and grounded in evidence. In weaker cultures, conversations shift toward assumptions, shortcuts, or personal preferences. Culture reveals itself in language.

Priya spent exactly five minutes at the opening of the Veridian calibration meeting setting norms. She had debated whether to do it at all—the leaders knew each other, the agenda was full, and she was aware that norm-setting can feel performative if it isn't done with conviction.

She decided the five minutes were not optional.

"We are here to see our people clearly," she said. "Not to rank them, not to protect our own teams, and not to sort people into categories that will follow them around for years. We're here to make sure every person in this organization has a fair shot at being seen for who they actually are. That means we'll ask each other for evidence. It means we'll challenge each other when we hear assumptions. And it means we'll be willing to change our minds. That is not a sign of weakness. That is the entire point of being in this room together."

She paused. "One more thing. The names we discuss today are real people with real careers. The way we talk about them in here will shape what happens to them out there. I'd ask everyone to hold that."

The room was quiet for a moment. Then Marcus said, simply, "Agreed." And the meeting began.

Those five minutes did something that no agenda item could have done: they established that this was a room where honesty was expected, where discomfort was acceptable, and where the standard was care rather than convenience. When the harder moments came—

when Rafael admitted he hadn't seen Camille's work, when the group pushed back on a placement, when Priya asked a question nobody wanted to answer—the norms held. Not because they were rules, but because they had been named out loud by someone with the authority to name them, in a room where everyone had agreed.

Culture is built in moments like this. Small ones, deliberate ones. The five minutes Priya spent at the beginning of that meeting were worth more to Veridian's talent culture than any policy document the company had ever written.

CHAPTER NINE

Facilitating a Talent Review That Works

Great Talent Reviews don't happen by accident. Someone has to build the conditions that make honesty possible.

Facilitation isn't about controlling the conversation or being the loudest voice in the room but instead guiding leaders through a structured, fair, and intentional process. It calls for confidence, curiosity, emotional intelligence, and a calm center: a good facilitator not just running the meeting but protecting it—along with the clarity, fairness, pace, purpose, people, and integrity of decisions made.

It begins long before the meeting starts with sound preparation: reviewing talent profiles, organizational structures, succession charts, readiness assessments, performance data, and strategic priorities. Facilitators who prepare thoroughly walk in with confidence and can anticipate questions, offer context, and keep the conversation grounded.

Once the meeting begins, the facilitator's first job is to set expectations so leaders understand meeting goals, the structure of the conversation, time boundaries, and norms guiding how to speak about people. Facilitators set the tone by naming what matters: honesty, evidence, respect, fairness, shared ownership, and clarity.

When it comes to the conversation itself, the facilitator is part conductor, part coach, part guardrail. They guide pace, clarify language so vague statements become specific and actionable, and interrupt bias not with accusation but with curiosity. They also ask for evidence, redirect unhelpful commentary, ensure leaders evaluate based on the same standards, and notice patterns—who's being praised or overlooked, where the group is getting stuck—to adjust the conversation accordingly.

One of the most important facilitation skills is asking good questions:

- "Can you give an example of that behavior?"
- "What opportunities has this person had to demonstrate readiness?"
- "Is this based on performance or visibility?"
- "What would help them grow in this area?"
- "Has their development progressed since the last review?"

Another critical skill is redirecting with grace. A strong facilitator steps in gently but firmly when a leader offers unhelpful commentary—personality judgments, assumptions about intent, or comments based on style rather than substance—asking things like: "Let's focus on observable behavior," "Let's talk about what we know instead of what we assume," or "Let's shift back to the strengths and evidence gathered."

One of a facilitator's most valuable contributions is pattern recognition: noticing when high performers are concentrated on one team, when specific demographics are underrepresented in high-potential categories, when succession gaps are in play, or when retention risks cluster in particular departments.

As the meeting draws to a close, facilitators close the loop: summarizing decisions, confirming next steps, assigning owners, and setting timelines. After the meeting, they support leaders by shaping development plans, identifying opportunities for exposure, recommending training resources, and partnering to ensure follow-through.

What Facilitation Sounds Like in the Room

Sometimes the easiest way to understand good facilitation is to hear it. The following composite example shows how a conversation can drift into assumption and how a facilitator can bring it back to evidence without shaming anyone in the room.

> **Leader A:** *I have Jordan as solid performance, lower potential. I just don't see executive presence yet.*
>
> **Facilitator:** *Let's pause on the phrase 'executive presence.' What specific behavior are we describing?*
>
> **Leader A:** *Jordan is quiet in senior meetings and does not jump in quickly.*
>
> **Leader B:** *That's true in live meetings, but Jordan's written analysis is usually the clearest material we receive before decisions are made.*
>
> **Facilitator:** *That distinction matters. Are we evaluating strategic thinking, communication style, or comfort with senior-room dynamics?*
>
> **Leader A:** *Probably comfort with the room.*
>
> **Facilitator:** *Great. Then the development need may not be potential. It may be exposure, coaching, and practice presenting recommendations verbally. What evidence do we have about Jordan's actual judgment and learning velocity?*

Leader C: *Jordan led the inventory recovery project and identified the root cause faster than anyone expected. The team adopted their process.*

Facilitator: *So let's capture that clearly: strong analytical judgment, proven process improvement, needs more senior-level presentation reps. Does that change the placement or the development plan?*

That is the work. The facilitator does not embarrass the leader, overrule the room, or pretend the concern does not exist. Instead, they translate vague language into observable behavior, separate style from capability, and turn a label into a development action.

The Derailed Version

Here is the same conversation without a skilled facilitator:

Leader A: *Jordan does not have executive presence.*

Leader B: *Agreed.*

Facilitator: *Okay, lower potential. Moving on.*

That version is faster, but it is not fairer. It creates a career-shaping conclusion without evidence, context, or a development path. A good facilitator protects the process from exactly this kind of shortcut.

When There Is No Dedicated Facilitator

Not every organization has a trained HR business partner available to facilitate Talent Review. In smaller companies, growing teams, or resource-constrained environments, the person who runs the Talent Review meeting may also be the person who prepared the talent profiles, manages the HRIS system, and handles employee relations.

That is reality for many leaders — and it does not have to mean a worse process. It means a different kind of preparation.

The first option is peer facilitation: designating one leader in the room to hold the facilitation role for the session. This works best when the designated facilitator is not the most senior person in the room (seniority tends to suppress challenge), has read the facilitation chapter in advance, and is freed from advocating for their own team during the meeting so they can focus on the room. Rotate the role each cycle so no one carries it permanently.

The second option is structured self-facilitation: replacing the live facilitator with a written agenda that does the guardrail work in advance. A well-designed agenda can enforce time limits, require evidence before placement, build in an equity review, and prompt calibration questions at each stage. The agenda becomes the facilitator. The discipline is in committing to follow it even when the conversation wants to move faster.

A basic self-facilitation agenda for a two-hour session might look like this:

- 0:00 — Norms and definitions (15 min): Align on what performance, potential, and readiness mean for your organization before discussing anyone.
- 0:15 — Individual discussions (60–70 min): For each employee, state the proposed placement, name the evidence, invite challenge, confirm or adjust. Time-box each person.
- 1:25 — Succession and equity sweep (20 min): Who is missing from the high-potential or succession list? Who has received the fewest opportunities? Name the gaps.

- 1:45 — Commitments and owners (15 min): Every development action gets a name and a date before the meeting ends.

The third option — and the right one when the stakes are high or the team is new to the process — is external facilitation. An outside HR consultant or organizational development practitioner brings the same skills as an internal HR partner without the organizational baggage. For an organization doing its first structured Talent Review, one externally facilitated session can establish norms, calibrate definitions, and model the process in a way that makes every subsequent session easier to run internally.

> *The goal of facilitation is not to have a perfect facilitator in the room. The goal is to have something — a person, an agenda, a set of norms — that protects the conversation from its worst instincts. That something can take many forms.*

Whatever form it takes, the non-negotiables remain the same: shared definitions before names are discussed, evidence required before placements are confirmed, bias named when it surfaces, and commitments documented before anyone leaves the room.

About an hour into the Veridian meeting, the group reached Jordan, a senior analyst in one of the mid-size departments. The department head, Trevor, presented Jordan as solid performance, lower potential. His reasoning: "I just don't see executive presence yet."

Priya recognized the phrase immediately. It was one of the most common pieces of vague language in any calibration room—useful-sounding, evidence-free, and frequently a cover for something else entirely.

"Let's pause on that phrase," she said. "'Executive presence' can mean a lot of things. What specific behavior are we describing?"

Trevor thought for a moment. "Jordan is quiet in senior meetings. Doesn't jump in quickly."

Kenji, who had worked with Jordan on a cross-functional project the previous year, leaned forward. "That's true in live meetings. But Jordan's written analysis is usually the clearest material we receive before any major decision. I've started circulating it to my own team."

Priya: "That distinction matters. Are we evaluating strategic thinking, communication style, or comfort with senior-room dynamics? Because those are different development needs."

Trevor paused. "Probably comfort with the room, if I'm honest."

"Then the development need isn't potential," Priya said. "It's exposure, coaching, and practice presenting recommendations verbally. What evidence do we have about Jordan's actual judgment and learning velocity?"

The room produced more. Jordan had led a project recovery that had saved a significant client relationship. Jordan had identified a process inefficiency before anyone else had seen it and had brought a solution alongside the problem. The pattern was consistent: strong thinking, quieter delivery.

"So let's capture this accurately," Priya said. "Strong analytical judgment, proven under pressure, needs senior-level presentation experience. Does that change the placement or the development plan?"

Trevor changed the placement. He also left the meeting with a specific commitment: to include Jordan in the next senior presentation to the executive team, with coaching beforehand.

On the drive home, Trevor thought about how close Jordan had come to leaving that room with a lower potential rating that had nothing to do with potential.

CHAPTER TEN

Post-Meeting: When the Real Development Happens

Insight means nothing without action—development lives in the follow-through.

The first (and most important) step is closing the feedback loop. Employees deserve to know where they stand, not in the form of labels or nine-box placements but via meaningful, human conversations about their strengths, opportunities, and potential. Post-Talent Review conversations should feel like a continuation of conversations leaders have all year so employees feel informed, encouraged, grounded, and clear about what comes next:

- An appreciation for strengths and contributions
- Clarity about what the organization sees in them
- An honest discussion of development areas
- An exploration of career aspirations
- Agreement on next steps
- Shared development plan ownership

On the heels of the conversation, leaders must transform insights into a development plan that's real—not vague, recycled, aspirational, or a list of tasks disguised as growth. Real development plans include three types of growth experiences:

1. Skill-building (what they need to learn)
2. Exposure (who they need to work with or learn from)

3. Experiences (what they need to lead or practice)

One of the biggest leadership mistakes? Confusing performance tasks with development opportunities. Development isn't about doing more—it's about doing things differently. Examples include:

- Asking employees to lead cross-functional projects rather than take on a heavier workload
- Having employees coach a peer or run a team meeting rather than train new hires
- Giving employees the chance to present to leadership rather than assigning them more tasks

A strong follow-through strategy also loops in sponsorship beyond mentorship. While mentorship develops a person, sponsorship opens doors—and the research consistently shows that access to sponsorship is unevenly distributed. A 2024 scoping review of sixteen studies found that women are less likely to be identified for or given access to sponsorship across nearly all organizational contexts examined.[4] Employees—especially women, people of color, introverts, and those in behind-the-scenes roles—often need someone with influence to advocate for them not because they are less capable, but because the systems that distribute visibility and advocacy are not neutral. Talent Review is one of the few structured moments when that imbalance can be named and acted on.

---

[4] Schwartz, R., Williams, M. F., & Feldman, M. D. (2024). Does Sponsorship Promote Equity in Career Advancement in Academic Medicine? A Scoping Review. *Journal of General Internal Medicine□: JGIM*, *39*(3), 470–480. https://doi.org/10.1007/s11606-023-08542-4

Follow-through also requires tracking progress in a developmental (not punitive) way, with leaders scheduling check-ins to ask:

- What's working well?
- What's been challenging?
- What have you learned?
- What support do you need?
- What's next?

The final follow-through piece is communicating the wins. When employees receive opportunities, leaders see growth, and development plans lead to promotions or expanded responsibilities, all of it deserves genuine recognition—not as a performative thing but to reinforce the value of the process and motivate leaders to stay committed.

Building Follow-Through Into the System

Behavioral reminders help. Manager coaching helps. But the most durable follow-through solution is a structural one: making it mechanically harder for commitments to disappear than to survive.

The most common reason development commitments fade is not that leaders stop caring — it is that the commitments live nowhere. They are not in any system. They are not on any calendar. They are not connected to any process that will surface them again. When that is the case, the next urgent thing will always win. The fix is to put the commitments somewhere that has memory.

Connect Talent Review to the Budget Cycle

Development commitments that require resources — training, conference attendance, coaching, backfill coverage for a stretch assignment — should be submitted to the budget process within thirty days of the Talent Review meeting. This is not a formality. It is a forcing function. If a development action has a budget line, it has a sponsor, a timeline, and an organizational record. If it does not, it is a wish.

HR leaders who want to institutionalize this should partner with Finance before the Talent Review cycle begins — not after. Agree on a submission window, a standard request format, and which categories of development spend require pre-approval. When leaders know their development commitments will be reviewed alongside headcount and capital requests, they make them with more intention.

Use Your Existing Project Management Infrastructure

Most organizations already have project management or task-tracking tools — whether that is Asana, Monday, Jira, Microsoft Planner, or a shared spreadsheet. Talent Review commitments should live in those systems, not in a separate HR document that only HR can see. When a leader commits to creating a stretch assignment for a specific employee by a specific date, that commitment should be a task with an owner, a due date, and a reminder. The tool does not matter. The discipline of using it does.

For organizations with an HRIS that supports goal-tracking or development plan modules — ADP, SuccessFactors, Workday, BambooHR, Lattice, 15Five, and others offer this — entering development commitments directly into the system creates a record that survives leadership transitions, surfacing automatically during performance cycles and enabling HR to track completion rates across the organization. This turns follow-through from a personal behavior into an organizational metric.

Tie Commitments to the Performance Review Calendar

If Talent Review happens in Q1, development plan progress should be a standing agenda item in Q2 and Q3 manager check-ins and a formal input to the Q4 performance review. When leaders know they will be asked about follow-through in a process that is already scheduled and consequential, the commitment has a deadline it did not have before. This is not surveillance — it is accountability built into rhythm.

HR can support this by sending a thirty-day and ninety-day pulse to managers after Talent Review — a simple two-question check-in: which commitments have been acted on, and which have stalled and why. The data tells HR where to coach and where to escalate. It also signals to leaders that someone is paying attention, which changes behavior more reliably than any training.

> *Follow-through is a behavior problem with a structural solution. When commitments live in systems that have memory, calendars that have accountability, and budgets that have owners, they survive the noise of daily work in a way that good intentions alone never can.*

None of this requires expensive technology or a large HR team. It requires agreeing, before the Talent Review meeting ends, on three things: where the commitments will be recorded, who will check on them, and when. That agreement — made in the room, in writing, with names attached — is the difference between a process that changes careers and one that generates paperwork.

Sound follow-through ultimately helps employees feel seen and supported, leaders feel confident, organizations thrive, and culture improve. Talent Review, after all, is only as good as what happens afterward.

Within a week of the meeting, Priya sent each of the six department heads a one-page summary: the employees they had discussed, the Now/Next placements, and the specific development commitments they had made in the room. The document was short by design. It was meant to be actionable, not archival.

She asked each leader to schedule employee development conversations within thirty days and to confirm with her when those conversations happened. She also built the commitments into Veridian's project management system—each action assigned to a named owner with a due date and a thirty-day reminder.

Most of the conversations happened. Rafael had his with Camille within the first week.

He told her that the leadership team had discussed her contributions. He told her specifically what they had seen—the Q3 discrepancy catch, the intake training she had built and run without being asked—and what they saw as her next development area. He told her the team believed she was ready for bigger scope and that he was going to make sure she had more visibility, starting with the next regional leadership briefing.

Camille was quiet for a moment after he finished. Then she said: "No one has ever told me any of this before. I didn't know anyone was paying attention."

Rafael reported the exchange back to Priya the following day. He seemed shaken by it in the way that good leaders are shaken when they realize what their inattention has cost someone. "I've been her manager for two years," he said. "She thought no one was paying attention."

"They weren't," Priya said. Not harshly—as a fact. "That's what we're changing."

That conversation—Camille's surprise, Rafael's reckoning—is the moment the entire process justified itself. Not the grid. Not the agenda. Not the definitions alignment or the norms-setting or the carefully constructed follow-through infrastructure. The moment when a leader looked at an employee and said, clearly and specifically: I see you. We see you. Here is what we see.

That is what Talent Review is for.

CHAPTER ELEVEN

Building Momentum All Year Long

Talent Review isn't an annual event but a continuous leadership habit.

Momentum transforms Talent Review from a process into a leadership habit and keeps development fresh, leaders engaged, and employees supported. This doesn't require more meetings or heavier processes but instead intention, rhythm, visibility, and follow-through as part of the normal course of leadership.

The first step? Weaving regular development check-ins into leadership routines—not heavy or formal conversations but simply as part of existing one-on-ones or project reviews to ensure development commitments don't gather dust.

Momentum also builds when leaders keep their eyes open for opportunities in real time. Leaders who keep Talent Review top of mind are quicker to say, "This would be a great opportunity for her" or "He's been wanting exposure in this area; let's bring him in." Such career-building moments create experience equity and prevent development from becoming something employees have to chase.

Another key piece: ongoing calibration, whether formal (once or twice a year) or informal (constantly). Monthly or quarterly "talent touchpoints" in leadership meetings help surface changes—a rising star making rapid progress, a developing leader struggling with confidence, a burnout risk, a new skill gained, a shift in career interests.

Momentum also grows when leaders recognize development both publicly and privately. In shouting out people who step up, stretch themselves, and take on new skills, leaders build confidence, encourage others to lean into development, and signal that Talent Review is not a secretive evaluation but a living, breathing part of how the organization grows its people.

Team-level insights should also shape leadership decisions directly. If the process identified a team lacks strategic thinking or needs stronger communication skills, leaders should build these needs into team meetings, training plans, and project assignments.

Leader modeling also comes into play. When leaders share what they're learning, where they're growing, or what they're practicing, it normalizes development for the entire team. A culture of development doesn't come from pushing people to grow but from leaders who grow openly themselves.

Reviewing progress at the leadership level on a quarterly basis—not full-blown Talent Reviews but something as simple as asking:

- Who's made noticeable progress?
- Who needs more support?
- Who's at risk of burning out?
- What development commitments have we fulfilled?
- Where have opportunities been unevenly distributed?
- What critical roles still lack successors?

These check-ins keep leaders aligned, the process honest, and development active.

Leaders also need to update talent profiles when significant changes occur—a new accomplishment, newly acquired skill, shift in career aspirations, or change in readiness. Keeping these profiles current arms leaders with accurate, up-to-date information rather than outdated impressions.

Finally, momentum is sustained when organizations consider Talent Review part of their business strategy instead of a seasonal HR event: using it to support hiring decisions, workforce planning, reorganization choices, leadership development efforts, and succession planning as a lens through which they view their teams.

Ninety days after the meeting, Priya sent a four-question pulse to all six department heads: Which commitments have you made progress on? Which have stalled, and why? What has changed about how you see your team? And what would you do differently in your preparation next time?

The responses were more honest than she had expected. Two leaders had followed through on every commitment. Two had followed through on most, with one item slipping in each case due to a reorganization that had consumed several weeks. One leader—Kenji—had exceeded his commitments, having not only delivered the promised development experiences but updated three talent profiles proactively when circumstances changed.

And then there was Elena.

Elena ran the largest team in the organization and was, by any operational measure, one of Veridian's strongest leaders. Her team delivered consistently. She was respected and, Priya knew, overextended. Her pulse response was two sentences: "I haven't had the development conversations yet. I'm not sure what I have to offer them right now."

Priya called her the next morning.

"Tell me what got in the way," Priya said.

Elena was quiet for a moment. "I didn't want to say 'we see potential in you' and then have nothing to back it up. My team is stretched. I don't have a stretch assignment to offer right now. I didn't want to make a promise I couldn't keep."

Priya understood this immediately. Elena was not avoiding accountability. She was avoiding the specific humiliation of raising someone's hopes without a concrete opportunity to follow through. It was a form of care that had been expressed as avoidance.

"The conversation is the opportunity," Priya told her. "Your people don't need a promotion in hand to feel seen. They need clarity. They need to know they're in the picture. That's what the conversation gives them—and you can give that right now, today, without a single open role to offer."

Elena had the conversations the following week. She reported back to Priya that two of her team members had seemed visibly relieved just to be told where they stood. "I kept waiting until I had something concrete," she said. "Turns out clarity was the concrete thing."

Darius's trajectory was tracking well by the ninety-day mark. He had been added to a cross-functional task force and given a presenting role at an upcoming client summit—both commitments made in the room by other leaders when Dominique had finally named what everyone had been quietly waiting to happen. He hadn't been told he was on the succession slate. He had been given the experiences that would make that slate credible when the time came. The difference, Priya reflected, was the difference between a promise and a plan.

When the Organization Is Not Ready Yet

Not every reader will work in an organization with polished talent systems, HR partnership, leadership buy-in, or a clean succession planning process. Some leaders are trying to do this work in messy, under-resourced, or inconsistent environments. If that is you, please hear this: you can still lead better from where you are.

Start small and local. Build talent profiles for your own team. Hold quarterly development conversations. Track strengths, aspirations, risks, and opportunities. Ask your peers how they define readiness. Share stretch assignments more intentionally. You may not be able to fix the whole organization, but you can create a more responsible process for the people within your reach.

Then document patterns. If your team lacks successors, if development opportunities are uneven, if critical roles have no backup, or if leaders are making inconsistent judgments, turn those observations into business language. Executives may not respond to "Talent Review feels broken," but they often respond to "We have three critical roles with no ready successors and no active development plan."

Finally, invite the organization forward instead of waiting for permission to care. A leader can pilot a simple talent conversation, test a one-page profile, or ask for thirty minutes with peers to calibrate definitions. Readiness does not always arrive before the work begins. Sometimes the work is what builds readiness.

When Your Workforce Includes a Bargaining Unit

Everything in this chapter assumes a degree of flexibility—the ability to assign stretch work, adjust roles, move people across teams, and build development experiences on the fly. Many organizations operate with significant constraints on all of those things. If your workforce includes employees covered by a collective bargaining agreement, this section is for you.

First, and most importantly: start with the collective bargaining agreement itself. If your CBA addresses talent assessment, development, promotion criteria, or succession processes for bargaining unit members—and many do, in varying degrees of specificity—that agreement is your framework. It is not an obstacle to good Talent Review practice. It is the floor the practice is built on. Follow it. Any talent process that operates outside or around the CBA, even with good intentions, creates legal exposure and erodes the trust that makes development conversations possible in the first place.

Where the CBA is explicit—on promotion sequencing, posting requirements, seniority provisions, or evaluation timelines—treat those provisions as design parameters, not complications. A well-run Talent Review in a unionized environment doesn't fight the agreement; it works within it to make the most of the latitude it provides.

Where the CBA is silent, the principles of this book apply—with an important scope adjustment. For most organizations with a mixed workforce, the most practical application of a structured Talent Review is to begin one level above the bargaining unit: with the frontline supervisors, team leads, and managers who sit just above the represented population. These are the leaders who directly shape the experience of every hourly or non-exempt employee beneath them, who are most likely to become your next level of middle management, and who are most often underdeveloped and under-reviewed despite carrying enormous organizational weight.

Starting here accomplishes two things. It keeps the talent process clean and legally uncomplicated, because you are working with nonrepresented employees where you have full flexibility. And it strengthens the layer of leadership that most directly affects the experience of your bargaining unit members—which is, ultimately, one of the most powerful ways to improve conditions for the represented workforce without touching the agreement at all.

If there is genuine appetite to build something that includes bargaining unit members, bring the union into the conversation before you build it. Not after. Not as a notification. As a partner in design. Union leadership understands the workforce in ways that HR and management often don't—what motivates people, what the actual development aspirations are, where the frustrations with the current system live. A talent process designed with union input is more likely to be trusted, more likely to be used honestly, and far less likely to become a grievance.

The development levers available in bargaining unit environments are different from those in a fully flexible corporate setting, but they are not absent. Cross-training, where permitted, builds skill breadth. Lead worker or team captain designations, where they exist in the agreement, can serve as structured stretch experiences. Joint labor-management committees offer a legitimate vehicle for conversations about workforce development that neither side can have alone. Tuition assistance and certification programs, common in many CBAs, are underused development tools in most organizations that offer them.

The goal in all of these environments is the same: see people clearly, develop them honestly, and build a pipeline that reflects actual talent rather than whoever happened to be most visible. The constraints are real. They are also navigable. And in every environment, unionized or not, the foundational leadership behavior that makes Talent Review meaningful is the same: paying attention to people all year long, not just during the process.

CHAPTER TWELVE

The Human Side of Things

Behind every name is a human being with a future worth honoring.

Talent Review happens behind closed doors. Its effects do not. Every decision made in that room — every placement confirmed, every development commitment logged, every name left off a succession slate — eventually reaches the person it was about. Not as a memo. Not as a meeting invitation. As a pattern of experience: who gets the stretch assignment, whose development conversation actually happens, whose manager advocates when a new opportunity surfaces.

Employees are remarkably good at reading these patterns. They may not know what was said in the Talent Review room, but they know whether they feel seen, whether their growth is being taken seriously, and whether the organization's stated values about people match what actually happens to them. That gap — between what organizations say and what employees experience — is where trust is built or broken.

The first human truth is this: employees want to be seen. Not praised indiscriminately — seen. They want evidence that someone has actually looked at their work, understands their strengths, and has a view on where they could go. A generic "keep doing what you're doing" conversation after a Talent Review is not evidence of that. A specific, honest, forward-looking development conversation is.

The second human truth: employees want direction, not ambiguity. In the absence of clarity, ambition curdles into frustration. Leaders who withhold honest feedback to avoid discomfort are not protecting their employees — they are leaving them to fill the silence with self-doubt and assumption. Clear, compassionate honesty is not harsh. It is one of the most useful things a leader can offer.

A hard truth: careless Talent Review practices—a lack of preparation, inconsistent standards, unexamined bias, or vague feedback—can do lasting damage to trust. Employees may not know the details, but they will feel the outcomes. And they will remember. Done with care, Talent Review builds the kind of loyalty no compensation package replicates. Done carelessly, it creates harm that takes years to repair.

Six months after the Veridian calibration meeting, Camille was leading a cross-regional implementation project—the largest scope she had been given in her four years at the company. She had been asked, not applied. The ask had come from Marcus directly, based on a conversation he had with Priya in which Priya had said, simply, "She's ready. Someone needs to give her the chance to prove it."

She was, by every visible measure, thriving. But the thing that had changed most was harder to observe from the outside. Camille had stopped assuming she was invisible. She had started bringing her thinking into rooms rather than waiting to be invited. She had started following up on her own ideas rather than waiting to see if anyone else would pick them up. She had started treating her own career as something worth advocating for.

None of that had happened because of a talent matrix. It had happened because one leader had sat across from her and said, with specificity and care: here is what we see in you, here is where we think you can go, and here is what we are going to do to help you get there. That conversation had lasted forty minutes. Its effects were still compounding.

Rafael had changed too. He had started scheduling monthly one-on-ones with the members of his team he knew least well. He had started asking about aspirations in those conversations, not just operational updates. He had started building profiles in his head all year rather than scrambling to complete them in the two weeks before the next Talent Review. He had not done any of this because he was told to. He had done it because the look on Camille's face when he told her the team had been discussing her contributions—the surprise, and then the quiet relief of it—was something he did not want to see again.

Camille's story is one story. In an organization of four hundred people, there are dozens of others. Some of them have managers like Kenji, who have been paying attention all along. Some of them have managers still learning to look. And some of them—and this is the hardest truth in any honest account of Talent Review—have managers whose limitations the process alone cannot fix. The conversation with Camille changed Rafael. Not every Rafael changes.

The process can create the conditions for that change. It cannot guarantee it.

What it can do is make it harder to walk out of the room without having seen someone clearly. That, over time, adds up to a culture.

CHAPTER THIRTEEN

A Note for the Person Being Reviewed

You are not a passive participant in this process. You never were.

Not as a consolation chapter. Not as an afterthought. As a genuine acknowledgment that Talent Review affects you deeply, that you have more agency in it than most organizations let on, and that knowing how this process works is one of the most useful things you can carry into your career.

I say this as someone who has been the talent under the microscope. I know what it feels like to wonder whether the people in that room can see you—really see you—or whether they're working from a partial picture, an outdated impression, or someone else's narrative about who you are. I also know what it feels like when they get it right: when a leader says "I see something in you" and means it, and follows through. It changes things. It changes you.

Here is what I want you to know: you are not simply waiting to be discovered. There are things you can do—before the meeting, after the meeting, and all year long—that meaningfully shape how you are seen, supported, and developed. None of them require you to be someone you're not. All of them require you to be intentional.

What Is Actually Happening in That Room

First, let's demystify the process. Talent Review is not a performance evaluation—that happens separately. It is not a ranking contest, a verdict on your worth, or a permanent label. It is a structured conversation in which your manager and other leaders discuss your contributions, your strengths, your development needs, and your potential. They are trying to figure out who is ready for what, where the gaps are, and how to invest in people's growth.

The people in that room are working from the information they have. Which means the quality of the conversation about you depends heavily on the quality of the information available—and some of that information comes from you, whether or not you realize it.

They are also working from their biases, their limited visibility, their assumptions, and whatever your manager says when your name comes up. A good process has checks on all of this. Not every organization has a good process. Knowing that is not meant to discourage you—it is meant to help you understand why showing up intentionally, all year long, matters as much as it does.

Before the Meeting: What You Can Do Now

The best time to shape how you are seen in a Talent Review is not the week before it happens. It is every week leading up to it. Here is what that looks like in practice.

Make your work visible. Not loudly, and not inauthentically. But if you are doing strong work that your manager cannot see—because it happens remotely, in a cross-functional project, or in a role without much senior exposure—you have a responsibility to surface it. Share updates. Summarize outcomes. When a project lands well, say so. This is not self-promotion; it is communication. The people evaluating your potential cannot advocate for what they don't know exists.

Tell your manager what you want. Leaders make assumptions about who wants what. If you have never said "I'm interested in taking on a bigger scope," "I'd love exposure to the senior leadership team," or "I'm thinking about where I want to grow in the next two years," your manager may not know. They cannot advocate for your aspirations if they don't know what they are. This conversation does not have to be formal. It can happen in a one-on-one. What matters is that it happens.

Ask to contribute to your talent profile. Many organizations now invite employees to contribute to their own profiles before Talent Review—sharing strengths, career interests, development goals, and key experiences. If your organization offers this, take it seriously. Do not write what you think they want to hear; write what is true and specific. If your organization does not offer this formally, ask your manager: "Is there anything I can share with you before Talent Review to make sure you have a full picture?" Most managers will welcome it.

Seek cross-functional visibility. One of the most powerful things that can happen in a calibration room is a second leader saying, "I've worked with them. Let me tell you what I've seen." You can increase the chances of that happening by raising your hand for cross-functional projects, volunteering to represent your team in broader forums, and building relationships outside your immediate department. The goal is not to network performatively; it is to ensure that more than one person in that room knows your work.

Find a sponsor—not just a mentor. A mentor gives you advice. A sponsor speaks your name in rooms you are not in. Think about which leaders in your organization have visibility into your work and have seen you handle something difficult well. Those are the people worth cultivating a relationship with—not transactionally, but genuinely. Leaders who believe in you and have influence are one of the most significant factors in whether your name comes up in Talent Review, and whether it is spoken with advocacy or afterthought.

After the Meeting: How to Have the Conversation You Deserve

After a Talent Review, your manager should reach out to have a development conversation with you. In a healthy organization, that happens within thirty days. In a less consistent one, it may happen months later, or not at all. If it does not happen on its own, you are allowed to ask for it. You are not being pushy. You are being a professional who takes their own growth seriously.

You might say: "I know Talent Review season has wrapped up. I'd love to find time to talk about my development—what you're seeing, where you think I'm growing, and what might be next. Can we put thirty minutes on the calendar?"

When that conversation happens, come with questions. Not to interrogate, but to engage. You deserve a real conversation—not a generic "keep it up." Here are questions that tend to open useful dialogue:

- "What do you see as my strongest contribution right now?"
- "Where do you think I have the most room to grow?"
- "What would 'ready for more' look like for someone in my role?"
- "Are there experiences or opportunities you think would help me develop in the areas you mentioned?"
- "Is there anything you think I should know about how I'm perceived that would be useful for me to hear?"

That last one takes courage. It is also often the most valuable question you can ask. Leaders who have honest information to share will appreciate being invited to share it. And if the answer is vague, you can follow up: "Can you give me a specific example?" You are not required to accept impressions as evidence. Neither is the room discussing you.

When the Feedback Is Hard to Hear

Sometimes the development conversation surfaces something difficult. A gap you weren't aware of. A perception you don't think is fair. A readiness assessment that stings. When that happens, try to stay in the conversation rather than shutting down or becoming defensive—not because the feedback is necessarily right, but because your response to it will itself be observed and remembered.

You are allowed to ask for more context: "Can you tell me more about what that looks like from your perspective?" You are allowed to share your own view: "That's helpful to hear. I'd push back gently on one part of it—can I share what I was seeing?" And you are allowed to take time to process: "Thank you for being honest with me. I want to sit with this and come back with some questions."

What you want to avoid is silence that looks like agreement, or defensiveness that closes the door on useful information. Both tend to work against you. The leaders who advance most consistently are often not the ones who receive the best feedback—they are the ones who respond to feedback with the most curiosity and resilience.

When the Process Does Not Feel Fair

Sometimes it won't. You may feel overlooked, mislabeled, or held to a different standard than a colleague. You may sense that your manager's limited visibility into your work has cost you. You may watch someone with less impact receive more opportunity because they are more visible, more similar to the leader, or better at advocating for themselves in ways that feel uncomfortable or unnatural to you.

These are real experiences. They are not imagined, and they are not your fault. Bias, inconsistency, and uneven access exist in every organization. The goal of a good Talent Review process is to reduce those things—not pretend they don't happen.

If you believe the process has been genuinely unfair, you have options. You can have a direct conversation with your manager: "I want to understand how I'm being evaluated and what factors are shaping that view." You can ask for a conversation with HR: "I have some questions about how Talent Review works and how I can make sure I'm being seen accurately." You can seek out a sponsor—a leader who knows your work and can advocate from the inside. And in some situations, you may need to decide whether this organization is one where your potential will actually be seen and developed—or whether your growth requires a different environment.

That last option is not defeat. It is self-awareness. Not every organization deserves you. The ones that do will show it—in how leaders talk to you, develop you, advocate for you, and follow through. Pay attention to that pattern. It tells you more about an organization's values than its mission statement ever will.

Own Your Development All Year Long

The final thing I want to say to you is this: do not outsource your development entirely to the organization. Leaders and HR partners play an important role—and this whole book has been about making them better at it—but your growth belongs to you.

Track your own wins. Keep a running document of projects you have led, problems you have solved, feedback you have received, and skills you have built. This serves two purposes: it grounds you when imposter syndrome creeps in, and it gives you specific, ready examples when someone asks what you've been working on—including in a talent profile.

Seek feedback before you need it. Do not wait for an annual review or a post-Talent Review conversation to find out how you are being perceived. Ask your manager regularly. Ask colleagues whose judgment you trust. Ask the leader of a cross-functional project you just completed. "What's one thing I could have done differently?" is a short question that produces some of the most useful information you will ever receive.

Hold your leaders accountable—gently but clearly. If a development commitment has gone quiet, follow up. "We talked about getting me involved in the next cross-functional initiative. I wanted to check in on where that stands." That is not demanding. That is partnership. Leaders who are serious about your development will welcome it. Those who are not will reveal themselves through their response—which is also useful information.

You deserve to be seen. You deserve development that is intentional and follow-through that is real. And you have more power to shape both of those things than you may have been led to believe. Use it.

When Veridian's second Talent Review cycle came around, Priya added something new to the preparation materials: a one-page invitation to employees to contribute to their own talent profiles before the meeting. Not required. Not evaluated. Just an invitation—a chance to share strengths, career interests, development goals, and experiences the manager might not have had direct visibility into.

Camille was the first to return hers.

She had written three paragraphs. The first described the cross-regional project she had led and what she had learned from it—specifically, what she'd found easy and what had stretched her. The second named two areas where she wanted to develop and why. The third said something Priya had not seen in a self-submitted profile before: "I know I've been hard to see in this role. I work independently and I don't tend to broadcast my work. I'm trying to get better at that. I wanted you to have the full picture before the meeting."

That last sentence was worth the entire initiative.

Camille had not written it because she was trying to manage her placement. She had written it because the previous cycle had shown her that the conversation about her happened whether or not she was in it, and that she had the ability to shape the information that conversation was built on. She had moved from passive subject to active participant—not by demanding a seat at the table, but by giving the room something true and specific to work with.

Rafael read Camille's profile three times before the meeting. He arrived, for the first time in his tenure at Veridian, fully prepared to advocate for someone he now understood in full.

CHAPTER FOURTEEN

When Talent Review Goes Sideways

A strong process is not proven by perfect conditions but by how leaders recover when the work gets messy.

Even when the intent is good, Talent Review can go sideways. Leaders arrive unprepared. A calibration disagreement gets tense. Someone uses vague language that carries bias. A development commitment never turns into action. An employee hears about a placement and feels reduced to a label. A reorganization wipes out the succession plan the team just built. None of these scenarios mean the process is doomed. They mean the process is real.

This chapter matters because practical leadership is not only about designing the ideal Talent Review. It is about knowing what to do when the ideal version meets human behavior, organizational pressure, and imperfect information.

When a Leader Refuses to Calibrate

Sometimes a leader walks into the room convinced their assessment is correct and remains unmoved by evidence. The facilitator's job is not to win an argument; it is to protect the standard of the process. Start by returning to the criteria: "What evidence supports this rating?" "Which examples show readiness?" "Where have we seen this behavior across more than one context?" If the leader still resists, separate the decision from the development action. The room may not fully agree on placement, but it can still agree on what evidence is missing and what experience the employee needs next.

> *"We are not aligned yet, so let's document the disagreement, identify the evidence needed, and revisit after the employee has had a fair opportunity to demonstrate the skill in question."*

This keeps the conversation from becoming a power struggle and turns uncertainty into a plan.

When a Bias Interruption Backfires

Bias interruptions can feel personal if the room has not practiced them. A leader may become defensive or worry they are being accused of bad intent. When that happens, slow the room down and re-anchor the purpose: "This is not about blame. It is about making sure we are using evidence and giving every employee a fair read."

Then translate the concern into process language. Instead of "That sounds biased," try "Let's separate communication style from impact" or "Let's check whether this employee has had the same opportunity to demonstrate readiness." The goal is to make the truth easier to hear so the group can act on it.

When an Employee Discovers Their Placement

Many organizations do not share box placements or internal succession labels with employees, and for good reason: labels can flatten a complex conversation into a single, emotionally loaded conclusion. Still, employees sometimes hear things informally or infer where they stand. When that happens, leaders should not hide behind process language.

The recovery conversation should focus on clarity, not the label: "I'm sorry this reached you in a way that felt confusing or discouraging. What matters most is that we talk about your strengths, your goals, what we see as the next development steps, and how I will support you." The repair comes from honesty and action, not secrecy.

When Follow-Through Falls Apart

The most common Talent Review failure happens after the meeting: the commitments simply fade. No one means for this to happen. Calendars fill, priorities shift, leaders move roles, and development promises become good intentions with no owner.

Recovery requires naming the miss quickly. "We committed to creating exposure in this area, and we have not done that yet" is a powerful sentence because it restores accountability without drama. From there, reset the plan with a named owner, a timeline, and a check-in date. Development plans are allowed to change; they are not allowed to evaporate.

When the Business Changes the Plan

Reorganizations, budget constraints, new strategies, leadership turnover, and market shifts can make a succession plan outdated almost overnight. That does not mean the Talent Review was wasted. It means the organization now has better information for the next decision.

When the business changes, revisit three questions: Which assumptions are no longer true? Which people are still ready, but for a different kind of opportunity? Which development needs became more urgent because the organization changed around them? Talent Review should be a living practice, not a laminated document.

A Simple Recovery Rhythm

When Talent Review goes sideways, use a simple rhythm: pause, name, ground, repair, and revisit.

- Pause long enough to stop the shortcut.
- Name what is happening without blame.
- Ground the room in criteria, evidence, and intent.
- Repair the action plan with a clear owner and timeline.
- Revisit the issue so the same failure does not become a pattern.

The healthiest organizations are not the ones where Talent Review never gets messy. They are the ones where leaders know how to notice the mess, learn from it, and come back to the people with more clarity and care than they had before.

Veridian's first structured Talent Review was not a success story. It was a start.

One leader arrived underprepared and spent the first twenty minutes of discussion recovering ground he should have covered in his profiles. The time cost was real—two employees who deserved full conversations got shorter ones because the group was already behind schedule. Priya noted it in her debrief and built profile quality coaching into the next preparation cycle. But those two employees had still been shortchanged, and no retrospective could undo that.

Elena's three-month delay on her development conversations was the follow-through failure that sat heaviest. Her reasons were real—the team was stretched, the timing was difficult, the fear of overpromising was genuine. But three of her team members had gone through the entire cycle without a development conversation, without knowing where they stood, without any of the clarity the meeting had been designed to produce. For them, the Talent Review had not happened at all.

There was also a harder miss: one employee—a mid-level project manager named Theo in Dominique's group—had been discussed briefly, placed in Needs Targeted Development, and assigned a development action that never materialized. Not because no one intended to follow through, but because the action had been assigned to a shared project infrastructure rather than to a named individual, and it had slipped through the gap. Theo had a review conversation that was warm and encouraging and vague. He left it without clarity. He left Veridian four months later.

Priya brought all of this to the second-cycle planning meeting. Not as an indictment, but as the curriculum. "We know where we broke down," she told Marcus. "Let's build those breakdowns into what we teach leaders to watch for."

That is the only honest posture available after a Talent Review goes sideways. Not defense of the process. Not blame of the leaders. A clear-eyed account of what failed, why it failed, and what structural change would make the same failure less likely next time. The process is only as good as what the organization learns from running it.

CHAPTER FIFTEEN

Bringing It All Together

The point was never to put people in boxes. The point was to make sure leaders stop using invisible boxes without realizing it.

If you have made it this far, you have walked through the full arc of Talent Review: why it exists, how it drifted, what the tools can and cannot do, where bias hides, how calibration creates fairness, why visibility and exposure matter, what leaders own, how culture shapes the room, what facilitators protect, why follow-through is the real test, how momentum keeps the work alive, and what to do when the process gets messy.

That is a lot. And still, the heart of the work is simple: see people clearly, talk about them responsibly, and do something useful with what you learn.

Talent Review becomes meaningful when it changes leadership behavior. Not when the grid is completed. Not when the meeting ends. Not when the succession chart looks tidy. It becomes meaningful when a leader leaves the room and has a more honest development conversation. When someone overlooked gets a stretch opportunity. When a vague concern becomes a coaching plan. When a successor is prepared before the emergency. When a team realizes the same few people have been receiving every opportunity and decides to change that pattern.

> *That is the real measure of this work: not whether leaders can discuss talent, but whether employees experience better leadership because of the discussion.*

So here is the closing charge: do not let Talent Review become theater. Do not let the form do the thinking. Do not let comfort make the decision. Do not let a single leader's view become someone's entire story. Do not let development plans become polite fiction.

Use the tools, but do not worship them. Use the structure, but do not hide behind it. Use calibration, but do not weaponize consensus. Use succession planning, but remember that names on a chart are people with real careers, real hopes, and real consequences attached to the decisions made about them.

And while we are talking about succession planning — let's be clear about what is actually at stake. The average cost of an unplanned leadership vacancy runs between 50 and 200 percent of the departing leader's annual salary, once you account for recruiting, lost productivity, team disruption, and the institutional knowledge that walks out the door. Organizations with weak talent pipelines are slower to respond to market shifts, more vulnerable to key-person risk, and more likely to promote reactively — installing the person who happened to be available rather than the person who was ready. A Talent Review process done well is not a team-building exercise. It is a risk management strategy. It is how organizations avoid being caught flat-footed when a critical role opens, a high performer leaves, or a new direction demands capabilities the current bench does not have. The human approach and the business case are not in tension here. They are the same argument. Leaders who see their people clearly, develop them intentionally, and build honest succession plans are not being soft. They are being prepared.

The best Talent Review practice is not colder because it is structured. It is kinder because it is structured. It gives leaders a way to slow down, question assumptions, compare evidence, share responsibility, and make commitments that actually help people grow.

That is what it means to unbox talent: to remove the lazy labels, open up the conversation, and make room for the full person to be seen.

Talent Review is a framework. Leadership is the force.
But the legacy is what happens next: the conversation you have, the opportunity you create, the assumption you challenge, the employee you sponsor, the promise you keep.

Veridian's second Talent Review cycle opened differently than the first.

The prep calls were shorter because the leaders already knew what they were preparing for. Three of the six submitted profiles that Priya would have held up as models—detailed, evidence-based, with employee contributions folded in. The definitions of performance, potential, and readiness were not relitigated in the meeting because they had been agreed on the year before and had survived intact. The Now/Next categories felt familiar in the room in a way that meant the group could spend its energy on the people rather than the tool.

There were still hard moments. A new department head who had joined six months earlier was underprepared and knew it—she said so at the start of the meeting, which was itself a sign of something changing in the culture. The succession slate was still thinner than it should have been in two departments, a problem that one year of better process could not fully repair.

But Darius presented to the executive team at the client summit. His sponsor—a senior leader who had raised his hand in the first cycle—had spent three sessions with him beforehand, not reviewing his slides but asking him hard questions about his thinking and letting him find his way to better answers. The presentation landed well. Marcus mentioned it in the all-hands meeting the following week.

Camille's profile was the strongest in the operations group. Rafael had not needed Priya to remind him to prepare it. He had been keeping notes since January.

Elena arrived with every commitment from the previous cycle completed and documented. She had not waited for the pulse survey to surface the ones that had slipped. She had caught them herself, had conversations about them, had reset timelines and followed through. She came into the room, as she later told Priya, feeling like she actually deserved to be there.

This is what a talent culture looks like in the making. Not a perfect process. Not leaders who never fall short. A room full of people who have done this before, who understand what they're trying to do and why it matters, who have seen what it looks like when it works—and who have enough of the right habits built into their rhythms that the process runs cleaner the second time than the first.

Veridian is not a finished story. The third cycle will surface new problems. A leader will leave and take institutional knowledge with them. A succession plan will be upended by a reorganization. An employee who was seen clearly in one cycle will feel overlooked in the next. These things happen in every organization because organizations are made of people and people are complicated and the work is never done.

But Camille knows someone is paying attention. Darius has a sponsor. Elena knows how to have the conversation. Rafael knows what a complete profile looks like and why it matters. The definitions are shared. The commitments have a home.

That is not the end. That is a foundation. And a foundation, built on intention and care and the willingness to look honestly at what works and what doesn't, is exactly where every meaningful culture begins.

Now go build the kind of process your people can feel—even if they are never in the room.

With cheer and receipts,
Your Corporate Cheerleader

BONUS CHAPTER

The Leader's Self-Assessment

You can't lead a fair Talent Review if you don't know where you're starting from.

Before you walk into a Talent Review room—or before you complete a talent profile, or before you have a development conversation—there is one more person worth evaluating: yourself.

This isn't about self-criticism or finding things to feel bad about. It's about honest awareness. The leaders who do Talent Review well aren't the ones who are free from bias or perfectly prepared every time. They're the ones who know where they tend to fall short and make intentional choices because of that knowledge.

This self-assessment is designed to help you do exactly that. It has five sections: how well you know your people, where your biases tend to show up, how you handle difficult conversations, how equitably you distribute opportunity, and how accountable you are to follow-through. There are no right answers. There is only honest reflection—and what you decide to do with it.

Take your time with this. Write in the spaces. Come back to it after your next Talent Review and see what has changed.

Rate yourself on each item using the scale below.

1 = Rarely or never 3 = Sometimes 5 = Consistently and confidently

Section 1: Knowing Your People

Great Talent Review starts long before the meeting. It starts in the hallway, in one-on-ones, in the moments leaders choose to pay attention. This section asks how well you actually know the people you're being asked to evaluate.

I can name each team member's top two or three strengths with specific examples. 1 2 3 4 5 *(circle one)*

I know what each person on my team wants next in their career. 1 2 3 4 5 *(circle one)*

I can describe each team member's growth over the past twelve months. 1 2 3 4 5 *(circle one)*

I know which team members feel most engaged—and which feel most at risk of leaving. 1 2 3 4 5 *(circle one)*

I have had at least one meaningful development conversation with each person in the last six months. 1 2 3 4 5 *(circle one)*

1. Where do you feel most confident in your knowledge of your team?

Name the person or people you feel you see most clearly—and what you know about them that others might not.

2. Where is your knowledge thinnest?

Is there someone on your team you'd struggle to advocate for in a calibration room? What has made it hard to know them better?

REFLECTION PROMPT

If you had to describe each team member's potential to a room of leaders who had never met them, could you do it? Not their job title or their tasks—their potential. If the answer is "not for everyone," that is important information. It doesn't mean you're a bad leader. It means you have work to do before the meeting.

Section 2: Understanding Your Biases

Every leader has bias. The ones who do the most damage in Talent Review are not the leaders with the most bias—they are the leaders who believe they have the least. This section is not designed to make you feel accused. It's designed to help you see clearly.

I evaluate people based on observable behavior and evidence, not gut feeling alone. 1 2 3 4 5 *(circle one)*

I am aware of which team members I feel most comfortable with—and I account for that. 1 2 3 4 5 *(circle one)*

I actively question whether someone's quietness, communication style, or work arrangement is affecting my perception of their potential.

1 2 3 4 5 *(circle one)*

I can think of a time I changed my mind about someone based on new evidence. 1 2 3 4 5 *(circle one)*

I notice when I'm using the word "confident" or "presence" without being able to define what I actually mean.

1 2 3 4 5 *(circle one)*

3. Which bias do you think shows up most in how you evaluate people?

Like-me bias, proximity bias, recency bias, confidence bias, halo/horn effect—or something else entirely.

4. Can you think of a time bias affected a decision you made about someone on your team?

You don't have to share this with anyone. But naming it honestly is the beginning of changing it.

REFLECTION PROMPT

Think of the person on your team you advocate for most naturally and enthusiastically. Now ask yourself: Is it because of their results, or because of how much I enjoy working with them? Both can be true—but it's worth knowing which is driving the advocacy.

Section 3: Handling Difficult Conversations

One of the most important things Talent Review asks of leaders is honesty—not cruelty, but clarity. This section examines how comfortable you are delivering feedback that is real, specific, and sometimes hard to hear.

I give feedback that is specific and actionable, not vague or overly gentle. 1 2 3 4 5 *(circle one)*

When someone is underperforming, I name it directly rather than hoping they figure it out. 1 2 3 4 5 *(circle one)*

I follow up on difficult feedback to make sure the employee understood it and knows what support is available.

1 2 3 4 5 *(circle one)*

I am comfortable saying "I don't know" or "I was wrong" in a leadership conversation. 1 2 3 4 5 *(circle one)*

I have told a high performer something they didn't want to hear because it was true and useful. 1 2 3 4 5 *(circle one)*

5. What kinds of conversations do you tend to avoid or soften more than you should?

Think about the last time you gave feedback that was less direct than it needed to be. What held you back?

6. What would help you feel more equipped for the harder conversations Talent Review requires?

Coaching, language, practice, a thought partner—what do you actually need?

REFLECTION PROMPT

Vague feedback is not kindness. When you tell someone they're "doing great" when they actually need to grow in two specific areas, you are protecting yourself from discomfort at their expense. They leave the conversation without the clarity they need to improve. Clear, compassionate honesty—even when it's hard—is one of the most generous things a leader can offer.

Section 4: Distributing Opportunity Equitably

This is often the section that surprises leaders the most. Most of us believe we distribute opportunity fairly. The data—and honest reflection—often tells a different story. This section asks you to look at the patterns, not the intentions.

I consciously vary who receives stretch assignments, high-visibility projects, and leadership opportunities. 1 2 3 4 5 *(circle one)*

I can name someone on my team who has been underexposed—and I'm doing something about it. 1 2 3 4 5 *(circle one)*

I advocate for team members in rooms they are not in. 1 2 3 4 5 *(circle one)*

I think about whether remote, part-time, or less-visible employees have the same access to development as others. 1 2 3 4 5 *(circle one)*

I sponsor, not just mentor: I open doors, not just give advice. 1 2 3 4 5 *(circle one)*

7. Look at the last five significant opportunities you assigned or recommended. Who received them?

Write the names. Then ask: Is this the full range of potential on my team, or the familiar range?

8. Who on your team most needs an advocate right now—and what are you prepared to do about it?

Advocacy is not a feeling. It is an action. What is the specific next step?

REFLECTION PROMPT

Sponsorship is the most powerful thing a leader can offer and the least consistently given. Mentorship says "I believe in you." Sponsorship says "I said your name in a room you weren't in." Think about which team members have sponsors—and which are quietly waiting for someone to notice them.

Section 5: Following Through

Everything in this book has built toward this: Talent Review is only as good as what you do after the meeting. This section is the one to return to ninety days from now and answer again.

When I make a development commitment, I follow through on it.
1 2 3 4 5 *(circle one)*

I track what I've committed to and check in on progress regularly.
1 2 3 4 5 *(circle one)*

When a commitment stalls, I name it quickly and reset—rather than hoping no one notices. 1 2 3 4 5 *(circle one)*

My team members know that when I say something in a development conversation, it will happen. 1 2 3 4 5 *(circle one)*

I treat Talent Review as an ongoing practice, not a once-a-year event.
1 2 3 4 5 *(circle one)*

9. Think about the last development commitment you made to someone on your team. What happened?

Did it happen? If not, why not—and what did you do about the gap?

10. What is one concrete commitment you are prepared to make—right now, before your next Talent Review—to develop someone on your team?

Name the person. Name the action. Name the timeline.

REFLECTION PROMPT

The most trust-eroding thing a leader can do is make a commitment in a development conversation and then let it disappear. Employees remember. They may not say anything. But they adjust their expectations of you accordingly—and the next time you tell them something promising, they will believe it a little less. Follow-through is not a nice-to-have. It is the currency of leadership credibility.

Reading Your Results

Add up your ratings across all five sections. The maximum score is 125 (25 questions × 5 points each). But the number itself matters less than the pattern. Look at where you scored lowest—not to judge yourself, but to prioritize.

Score Range	What It May Indicate
100–125	You are operating with strong Talent Review habits. Your focus should be on sustaining consistency and coaching others to develop the same practices.
75–99	You have a solid foundation with specific areas to strengthen. Identify your two lowest-scoring sections and choose one concrete action in each before your next Talent Review.
50–74	You have meaningful growth opportunities ahead. This is not a criticism—most leaders fall here the first time they take an honest look. Pick one section to focus on in the next ninety days.
Below 50	This is a starting point, not a verdict. The leaders who ultimately do this work best are often the ones who began with the most honest assessment of where they were. You are in exactly the right place.

Your Pre-Talent Review Commitment

Before you close this chapter, write three things: one thing you will do differently in your preparation, one bias you will actively watch for in the room, and one person you commit to advocating for more intentionally in the next cycle.

I will do this differently in my preparation:

I will watch for this bias in the room:

I commit to advocating more intentionally for:

Come back to this page in ninety days. See what happened. Adjust. Repeat.

That is how leaders grow. Not in one big moment of insight, but in the small, sustained choices to see people more clearly, advocate more boldly, and follow through more consistently than the last time.

> *You don't have to be a perfect leader to do Talent Review well. You have to be a growing one.*

APPENDIX

Practical Tools and Templates

The following tools are intentionally simple. Use them as starting points, not sacred documents. Adapt the language to fit your organization, but keep the discipline: evidence, clarity, equity, ownership, and follow-through.

Tool 1: One-Page Talent Profile

Use this before the Talent Review meeting so the room has a shared, evidence-based view of the employee.

Section	Prompt
Employee snapshot	Role, tenure, current scope, manager, location/work arrangement.
Consistent strengths	What does this person reliably do well? Include examples.
Current impact	What results, relationships, processes, or outcomes are better because of this person?
Growth areas	What capability, exposure, or behavior needs development? Be specific.
Career aspirations	What does the employee want next? What have they actually expressed?
Potential indicators	What evidence suggests learning agility, adaptability, judgment, influence, or readiness for broader scope?
Readiness view	Ready now, ready soon, ready later, developing, or thriving in role. Include why.
Equity check	What opportunities has this person had or not had? What visibility gaps may exist?
Recommended next action	What development, exposure, sponsorship, or feedback should happen next?

Tool 2: Calibration Preparation Worksheet

Use this before calibration to help leaders arrive with evidence instead of impressions.

Question	Leader Notes
What are the clearest examples of this employee's performance over the past 6–12 months?	
What evidence supports the potential/readiness assessment?	
Where might I be relying on style, familiarity, proximity, or recency?	
What opportunities has this employee had that others may not have had?	
What opportunities has this employee not had yet?	
What feedback has the employee received, and how did they respond?	
What development action am I prepared to own after the meeting?	

Tool 3: Development Plan Structure

A development plan should be specific enough to guide action and flexible enough to evolve as the employee grows.

Element	Definition	Example
Development focus	The capability or experience to build.	Increase senior-level presentation confidence.
Action/experience	The stretch assignment, project, coaching, or exposure.	Present monthly operational insights to the leadership team.
Support needed	Manager, mentor, sponsor, training, time, or resources.	Manager reviews deck; sponsor provides feedback after presentation.
Evidence of progress	How growth will be observed.	Clearer recommendations, stronger executive Q&A, increased confidence.
Timeline	When the action starts and when it will be revisited.	Begin next month; review after three presentations.
Owner	Who is accountable for making the action happen.	Manager owns opportunity; employee owns preparation.

Tool 4: Post-Meeting Follow-Through Checklist

- Confirm final decisions, open questions, and unresolved calibration items.
- Assign an owner to every development commitment.
- Schedule employee feedback and development conversations.
- Update talent profiles, readiness notes, and succession risks.
- Identify stretch assignments, sponsors, mentors, or exposure opportunities.
- Check whether opportunities are equitably distributed across the team.
- Set a 30/60/90-day follow-up rhythm for development actions.
- Revisit commitments at the next leadership meeting or quarterly talent check-in.

Tool 5: Bias-Interrupt Question Bank

Bias Risk	Questions to Ask
Vague language	What specific behavior are we describing? What example supports that?
Like-me bias	Are we valuing similarity to the leader or actual capability?
Proximity bias	Would we assess this person the same way if they worked remotely or on another shift/site?
Recency bias	Are we overweighting the most recent event? What is the longer pattern?
Confidence bias	Are we mistaking polish or verbal speed for competence?
Visibility bias	Is this person less capable, or have they had less exposure?
Opportunity bias	Has this employee had the same access to stretch work, sponsorship, or feedback?
Halo/horn effect	Are we letting one strength or one mistake color the whole assessment?

Tool 6: Organizational Readiness Checklist

- Leaders share definitions of performance, potential, and readiness.
- Talent profiles are current and evidence-based.
- The organization has a process for calibration, even if simple.
- Development commitments have owners and timelines.
- Critical roles and succession risks are identified.
- Equity patterns are reviewed before decisions are finalized.
- Remote, hybrid, shift-based, and less-visible roles are considered intentionally.
- Leaders know what to do when the process breaks down.

Talent Models at a Glance

Full-page reference diagrams for all eight models covered in Chapter Three. Use these as conversation starters, not verdicts.

1. Nine-Box Grid

The most widely used model. Two axes — performance and potential — create nine distinct categories. Best for organizations new to structured Talent Review.

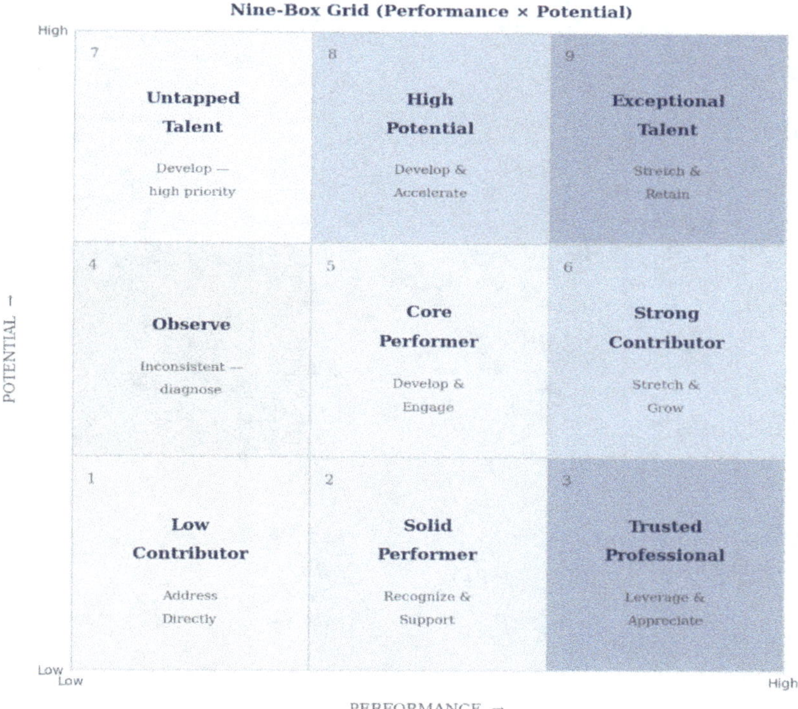

Nine-Box Grid — Performance × Potential

2. The 16-Box Model

An expanded version of the nine-box with four levels on each axis, allowing finer differentiation. Best for mature teams who need more nuance than the nine-box provides.

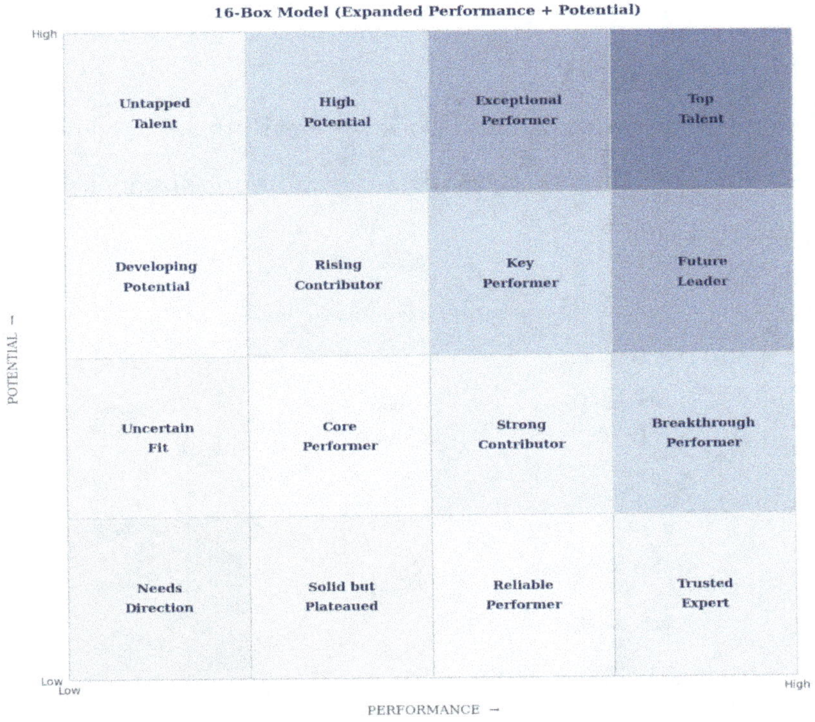

16-Box Model (Expanded Performance + Potential)

High

Untapped Talent
High Potential
Exceptional Performer
Top Talent

Developing Potential
Rising Contributor
Key Performer
Future Leader

Uncertain Fit
Core Performer
Strong Contributor
Breakthrough Performer

Needs Direction
Solid but Plateaued
Reliable Performer
Trusted Expert

POTENTIAL →

Low
Low
High

PERFORMANCE →

16-Box Model — Expanded Performance + Potential

3. Now/Next Model

A linear, conversation-first model asking two questions: where is this person now, and where might they go next? Best for leaders who find grids limiting.

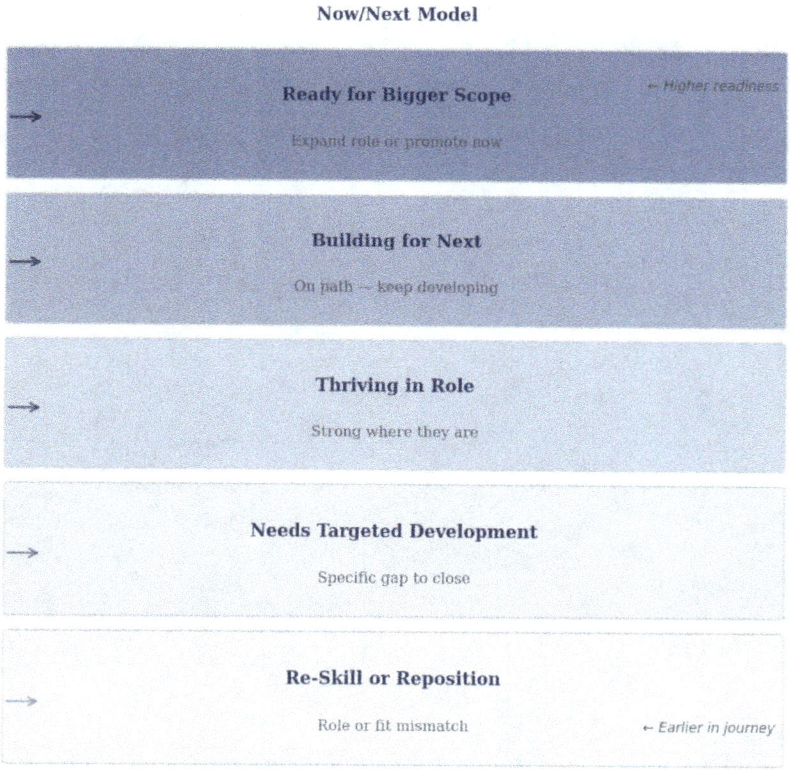

Now/Next Model

→ **Ready for Bigger Scope** ← Higher readiness
Expand role or promote now

→ **Building for Next**
On path — keep developing

→ **Thriving in Role**
Strong where they are

→ **Needs Targeted Development**
Specific gap to close

→ **Re-Skill or Reposition**
Role or fit mismatch ← Earlier in journey

Now/Next Model — Readiness and Direction

4. Impact/Potential Matrix

Replaces 'performance' with 'impact' — the actual effect someone has on results, people, and systems. Best for roles where output alone doesn't capture contribution.

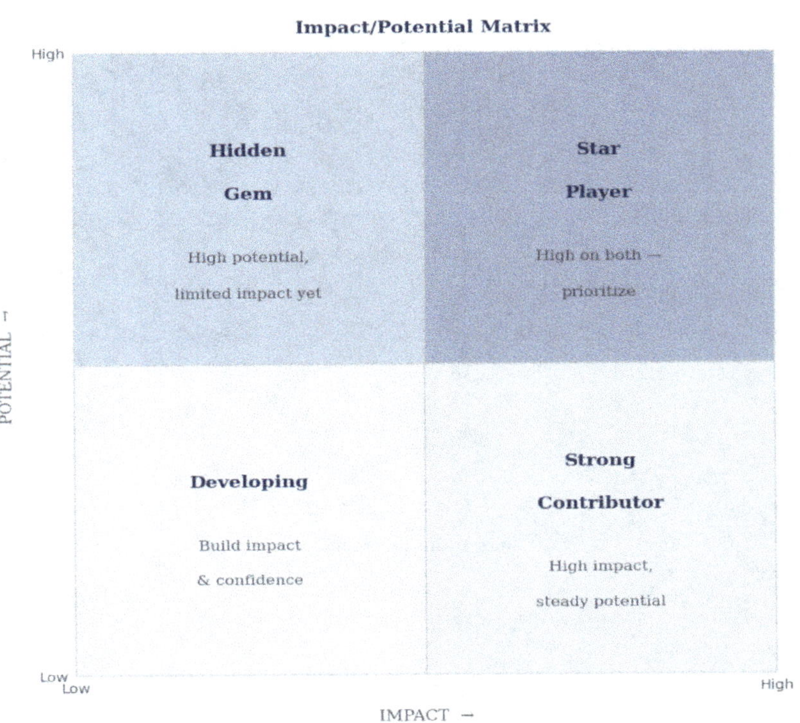

Impact/Potential Matrix

5. Growth Trajectory Model

Evaluates the direction and speed of development rather than a static placement. Best for fast-moving organizations where momentum matters as much as current performance.

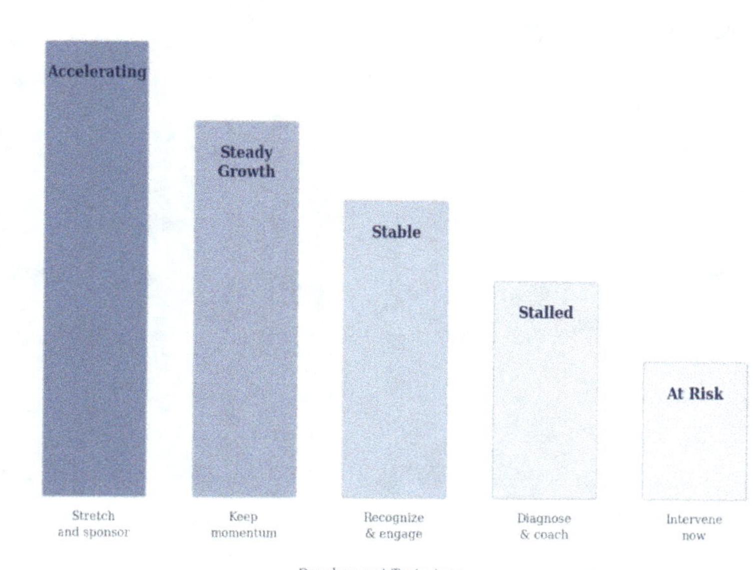

Growth Trajectory Model — Five Trajectory Categories

6. Narrative-Based Assessment

No grid, no box — just a structured written summary across six dimensions. Best for small, relational teams where nuance and context matter most.

Narrative-Based Assessment

Strengths
What this person does consistently well

Behaviors
How they show up and impact others

Contributions
Results and outcomes produced

Growth Areas
Where development is needed

Potential Indicators
Evidence of broader capability

Readiness Considerations
Timing and support for next opportunity

Narrative-Based Assessment — Six Dimensions

7. Capability-Future Potential Matrix

Uses the organization's competency model to evaluate current leadership behavior against future potential. Best for organizations with defined leadership expectations.

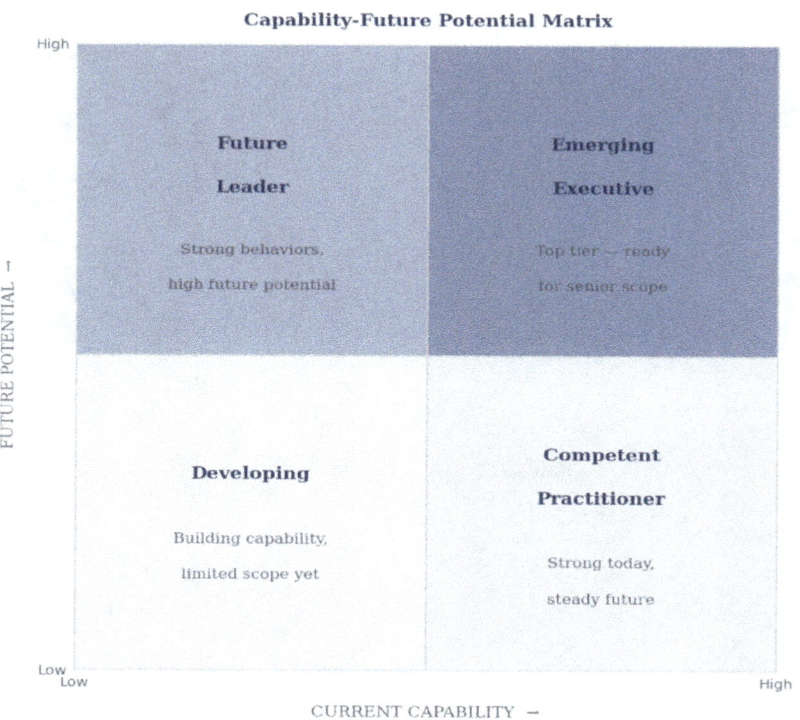

Capability-Future Potential Matrix

8. Flight Risk vs. Critical Value Matrix

A retention-focused model assessing how likely someone is to leave against how critical they are to the organization. Best used during periods of instability or high turnover.

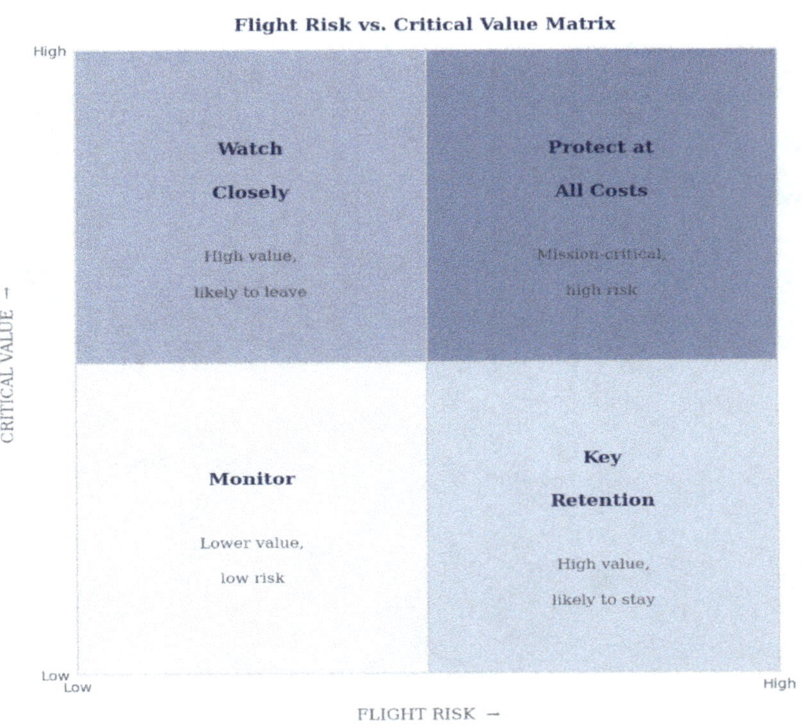

Flight Risk vs. Critical Value Matrix

APPENDIX

Glossary

Key terms used throughout this book, defined in plain language.

Calibration

A structured, facilitated conversation in which leaders align on shared definitions of performance, potential, and readiness before or after discussing individual employees. Calibration is the process by which individual opinions become collective standards. Without it, Talent Review is a collection of separate judgments that may or may not reflect the same criteria.

Capability-Future Potential Matrix

A talent model that evaluates an employee's current demonstration of leadership behaviors (based on an organizational competency model) against their potential for future roles. Requires that the organization have clearly defined leadership expectations to function.

Confidence Bias

The tendency to equate polished communication, verbal fluency, or visible self-assurance with actual competence or potential. One of the most common biases in Talent Review, and one of the most damaging to employees who lead in quieter, more deliberate ways.

Development Plan

A structured, actionable agreement between a leader and an employee that outlines the capability to build, the specific experiences or assignments that will build it, the support needed, and the timeline for revisiting progress. A real development plan is not a list of goals — it is a commitment with an owner.

Experience Equity

The intentional practice of distributing developmental opportunities — stretch assignments, high-visibility projects, leadership roles, sponsorship, and feedback — fairly across a team, rather than concentrating them among the most familiar or confident employees.

Facilitation

The act of guiding a Talent Review conversation with structure, fairness, and intention. A skilled facilitator sets norms, asks for evidence, interrupts bias, manages time, recognizes patterns, and closes the loop — without controlling the room or replacing leadership judgment.

Flight Risk vs. Critical Value Matrix

A retention-focused talent model that assesses both how likely an employee is to leave and how significant the loss would be to the organization. Used to prioritize retention efforts and succession investments during periods of instability or high turnover.

Follow-Through

The act of honoring commitments made during or after a Talent Review meeting — development conversations, stretch assignments, sponsorship actions, and development plan check-ins. The single most trust-building (or trust-eroding) leader behavior in the Talent Review cycle.

Growth Trajectory Model

A talent model that evaluates the direction and speed of an employee's development rather than their current standing. Categories typically include Accelerating, Steady Growth, Stable, Stalled, and At Risk. Best used in fast-moving environments where momentum matters as much as current performance.

Halo/Horn Effect

The tendency to allow one strong or weak attribute to color the entire assessment of an employee. A leader experiencing the halo effect may overlook significant development needs in a high-performing employee; the horn effect may cause a leader to underestimate someone recovering from a single visible misstep.

Impact/Potential Matrix

A talent model that replaces 'performance' with 'impact' — how meaningfully an employee influences results, people, systems, and culture. Useful in roles where metrics don't fully capture contribution, particularly in service, innovation, or collaborative environments.

Intent

In the context of Talent Review, the deliberate commitment to use the process for its original purpose: seeing people clearly, developing them honestly, and preparing the organization for what comes next. Without intent, Talent Review becomes a compliance ritual. With it, it becomes a leadership practice.

Like-Me Bias

The tendency to favor employees who share the leader's personality, communication style, background, or work approach. One of the most pervasive biases in talent evaluation, and particularly harmful in organizations with limited diversity at the leadership level.

Narrative-Based Assessment

A talent model without grids, boxes, or numerical ratings. Structured written summaries for each employee cover Strengths, Behaviors, Contributions, Growth Areas, Potential Indicators, and Readiness Considerations. Best for small, relational teams where nuance is more valuable than consistency at scale.

Nine-Box Grid

The most widely used talent model, plotting performance on one axis and potential on the other to create nine categories. A useful starting framework for organizations new to structured Talent Review, but prone to becoming a label system rather than a conversation tool when not well-facilitated.

Now/Next Model

A simple talent model built around two questions: Where is this employee now? And where might they go next? Categories include Ready for Bigger Scope, Building for Next, Thriving in Role, Needs Targeted Development, and Re-Skill or Reposition. Best for leaders and teams who find grids too rigid.

Performance

In Talent Review, what an employee has delivered and how consistently they have delivered it. Evidence of impact, reliability, problem-solving, and behavior. Performance is not proximity to the leader, likability, or volume of activity — it is observable, documented contribution over time.

Potential

In Talent Review, the likelihood that an employee will grow — and to what capacity — with the right support, experiences, and time. Potential is about trajectory, not current performance. It is measured through learning agility, adaptability, curiosity, and the ability to influence beyond one's immediate role — not charisma, confidence, or similarity to the leader.

Proximity Bias

The tendency to evaluate employees who are physically or organizationally closer to the leader more favorably than those who are remote, on different shifts, or in less-visible roles. A significant equity risk in hybrid and distributed organizations.

Psychological Safety

The degree to which leaders in a Talent Review room feel safe to be honest, ask questions, challenge assumptions, and change their minds without fear of judgment or retaliation. Without it, calibration becomes a performance rather than a conversation.

Readiness

A time-based assessment of an employee's preparedness to step into a larger role or take on expanded scope. Readiness is not a measure of worth — it is a measure of timing. Common readiness levels include Ready Now, Ready Soon (12–24 months), Ready Later (2–5 years), Developing, and Thriving in Role.

Recency Bias

The tendency to overweight recent events — a strong quarter, a public misstep, a tense interaction — at the expense of the longer pattern of an employee's contribution and growth. Particularly dangerous in annual Talent Review cycles where recency may dominate a twelve-month record.

16-Box Model

An expanded version of the nine-box grid, using four levels on each axis for sixteen total categories. Offers more precision than the nine-box and is better suited to large or highly differentiated organizations with experienced leadership teams who can navigate the additional complexity.

Sponsorship

The act of speaking an employee's name and advocating for their advancement in rooms they are not in. Distinct from mentorship, which develops the person, sponsorship opens doors. One of the most equity-producing actions a leader can take — and one of the most unevenly distributed.

Succession Planning

The strategic practice of identifying and developing employees who could step into critical roles if those roles became vacant. A living, evidence-based plan — not a static org chart. Strong succession planning answers: which roles are critical, who is ready, what experiences they still need, and where gaps remain.

Talent Profile

A structured, evidence-based summary of an employee's strengths, contributions, growth areas, career aspirations, and readiness. Used to prepare leaders for Talent Review conversations and to ensure the room has consistent, fair information about each employee before discussion begins.

Talent Review

A structured, intentional leadership practice in which leaders gather to assess performance and potential, calibrate standards, identify development needs, plan succession, and make equity-informed decisions about how to invest in the growth of their people. Not a performance review, not a ranking contest, and not a nine-box exercise — it is a leadership responsibility.

Visibility

The degree to which a leader is able to observe and understand an employee's contributions, strengths, and potential. Visibility is not a measure of performance — it is a measure of access. Employees with lower visibility are not necessarily less capable; they may simply have less exposure to the people making decisions about their futures.

APPENDIX

Frequently Asked Questions

The questions leaders actually ask — answered directly.

Do I have to use the nine-box?

No. The nine-box is a tool, not a requirement. It is the most widely recognized model because it is simple and visual, but it is also the most frequently misused — particularly when leaders treat box placements as permanent labels rather than conversation starters. If your team finds grids limiting, the Now/Next model or a narrative-based approach may serve you better. The goal is not to use a specific tool. The goal is to evaluate your people clearly and consistently. Choose whatever model helps you do that.

What if I don't have an HR partner to facilitate?

You can still do this. Without a dedicated HR facilitator, the responsibility for structure and norms shifts to whoever runs the meeting — often the most senior leader in the room, or a leader who has agreed to play the facilitation role for the session. Read the facilitation chapter carefully before the meeting. Set norms at the start. Ask for evidence. Interrupt vague language. The conversation will be less polished than one with a trained facilitator, but it will still be more fair and more useful than no calibration at all.

Can I share an employee's nine-box placement with them?

Most organizations do not share specific box placements, and there are good reasons for that. A placement is a moment-in-time assessment meant to guide a development conversation — not a permanent designation. Labels can flatten a nuanced conversation into a single emotionally loaded conclusion. What employees do deserve, however, is a clear, honest post-Talent Review conversation: what the team sees as their strengths, where development is needed, what their readiness looks like, and what comes next. The conversation is what matters. The box is a facilitation tool, not a verdict to be delivered.

What if a leader dominates the calibration room and won't change their assessment?

This is one of the most common facilitation challenges, and it rarely reflects bad intent. Leaders who dominate tend to be confident in their view and unpracticed at collaborative evaluation. The facilitator's job is not to overrule them — it is to keep returning to the criteria. Ask: 'What evidence supports that rating?' 'Where have we seen this behavior consistently across more than one situation?' 'Does the room agree?' If the leader still resists after the evidence conversation, name the disagreement directly and move on: 'We are not fully aligned here. Let's document it, note the evidence that would help us decide, and revisit after the employee has had a fair opportunity to demonstrate.' That approach protects the employee without creating a power struggle.

How often should we calibrate?

At minimum, once a year — but the organizations that do this best calibrate at least twice, with informal talent touchpoints in between. A formal mid-year check-in allows leaders to catch changes in readiness, flag emerging risks, update development commitments, and surface retention concerns before they become departures. Quarterly leadership conversations that include a brief talent component — even fifteen minutes — keep the work alive between formal cycles and prevent the annual review from being the only time leaders think about their people's growth.

What if our organization has no succession planning process?

Start with what you can control. You do not need an enterprise-wide succession program to identify your critical roles and ask who could step in if they became vacant tomorrow. Even a simple, informal conversation — 'Which three roles on this team would be hardest to fill, and who is developing toward them?' — is succession planning. Document the answers. Share them with your HR partner if you have one. Use them to drive development conversations. Over time, that informal practice becomes the evidence base for building something more formal.

Is it okay for employees to contribute to their own talent profiles?

Not only is it okay — it is strongly recommended. Employees who contribute to their own profiles bring information leaders may not have: career aspirations, development interests, skills the leader hasn't directly observed, and projects or contributions that happened outside the leader's line of sight. Employee-contributed profiles also reduce bias by grounding the room in the employee's own account of their work. The leader still owns the final profile and the Talent Review conversation — but the employee's voice in the preparation makes the assessment more accurate and more fair.

What do I do if I realize I've been consistently underestimating someone?

Name it. Not necessarily publicly in the calibration room, but in your own reflection — and then act on it. Schedule a conversation with the employee and acknowledge that you have not given them the visibility and opportunity their contributions deserve. Ask about their aspirations. Create a stretch opportunity. Speak their name in rooms they are not in. The most powerful thing a leader can do after recognizing a pattern of underestimation is to change the pattern — not with a dramatic gesture, but with sustained, intentional attention. Development delayed is not development denied, as long as the leader takes meaningful action once they see the gap.

How do I handle it when an employee hears about their placement and reacts badly?

With honesty and care — and without hiding behind the process. If an employee has heard about a placement informally or inferred where they stand, the leader's job is not to defend the system. It is to have a real conversation: about what the team sees as their strengths, what development is needed, and what the specific next steps look like. Acknowledge that learning about a placement without context is disorienting. Then provide the context. The repair does not come from explaining the process — it comes from demonstrating that the leader sees the employee clearly and is invested in their growth.

What is the single most important thing I can do to make Talent Review better?

Follow through. Everything else in this book — the profiles, the calibration, the bias interruptions, the succession conversations — depends on what you do after the meeting ends. Employees do not experience the Talent Review session. They experience the development conversation you have (or don't have), the stretch assignment you create (or don't create), the feedback you deliver (or withhold), and the promise you keep (or let fade). Follow-through is not one component of a good Talent Review practice. It is the proof that the practice is real.

Does this book apply to organizations with unionized or hourly workforces?

The principles do—the specific levers require adaptation. If your organization includes employees covered by a collective bargaining agreement, start with the CBA itself. Whatever it specifies about talent assessment, promotion criteria, or development processes for represented employees is your framework. Work within it, not around it. Where the agreement is silent, the principles in this book apply most cleanly to the layer of leadership just above the bargaining unit—the frontline supervisors, team leads, and managers who are most often underdeveloped and most directly shape the experience of the represented workforce. If there is genuine appetite to build something that includes bargaining unit members, bring union leadership into the design conversation before you build it. Chapter 11 covers this in more detail.

How does Talent Review connect to compensation decisions?

It doesn't—at least not directly, and not within the scope of this book. Compensation strategy is a distinct discipline with its own governance, legal considerations, and organizational politics. Conflating talent assessment with pay decisions in the same conversation tends to corrupt both: leaders begin managing their assessments to influence comp outcomes rather than to develop people accurately, and the calibration room stops being a place where honest conversations happen. This book is about seeing people clearly and developing them well. How that connects to your organization's merit cycle, long-term incentives, or equity grants is a conversation for your total rewards team—informed by, but separate from, the work described here.

What about HRIS and talent management software—how do I configure it to support this process?

This book deliberately does not prescribe specific platform configurations. HRIS systems vary enormously in capability depending on the package purchased, the implementation choices made, and the iterations each vendor has released since any guidance here was written. What works in one organization's Workday configuration may not exist in another's. The best source of guidance on how to map the Now/Next model, development plan structure, or follow-through tracking to your specific platform is your account executive or implementation partner—most major platforms have significant customization capability that goes unused simply because no one asked. Go ask.

www.ingramcontent.com/pod-product-compliance
Lightning Source LLC
LaVergne TN
LVHW010611110826
845149LV00003B/860

* 9 7 9 8 9 9 9 3 6 7 6 2 4 *